TOTAL CHAKRA
ENERGY PLAN

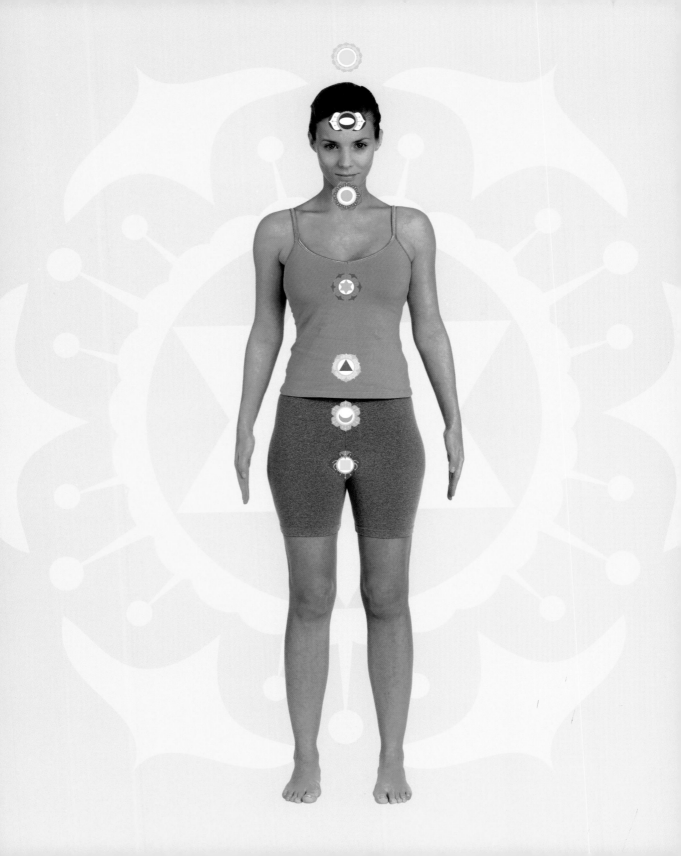

TOTAL CHAKRA ENERGY PLAN

*The practical 7-step
program to balance
and revitalize*

ANNA SELBY

DUNCAN BAIRD PUBLISHERS

LONDON

Total Chakra Energy Plan
Anna Selby

Distributed in the USA and Canada by Sterling Publishing Co., Inc.
387 Park Avenue South, New York, NY 10016-8810

This revised edition first published in the UK and USA in 2009 by Duncan Baird Publishers Ltd
Sixth Floor, Castle House, 75–76 Wells Street, London W1T 3QH

Library of Congress Cataloging-in-Publication Data

Selby, Anna.
   Total chakra energy plan : the practical 7-step program to balance and revitalize / Anna Selby. -- 1st ed.
      p. cm.
   Includes index.
   ISBN 978-1-84483-855-4
   1. Energy medicine. 2. Chakras--Health aspects. I. Title.
   RZ421.S45 2009
   615.8'51--dc22
                                    2009012692

10 9 8 7 6 5 4 3 2 1

ISBN: 978-184483-855-4

Typeset in Trade Gothic
Color reproduction by Scanhouse, Malaysia
Printed and bound in Malaysia for Imago

For information about custom editions, special sales, premium and corporate purchases, please contact Sterling
Special Sales Department at 800-805-5489 or specialsales@sterlingpub.com.

Publisher's note:
The information in this book is not intended as a substitute for professional medical advice and treatment. If
you are pregnant or are suffering from any medical conditions or health problems, it is recommended that you
consult a medical professional before following any of the advice or practice suggested in this book. Duncan
Baird Publishers, or any other persons who have been involved in working on this publication, cannot accept
responsibility for any injuries or damage incurred as a result of following the information, exercises, recipes or
therapeutic techniques contained in this book.

Dedication

For Philip and Christian, as ever

CONTENTS

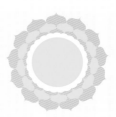

Introduction to the Chakras

Each and every one of us, as well as every other being, sentient or otherwise, on this planet, is composed of energy. This is a fact only recently realized by science, but it has been understood for millennia by mystics. Most ancient forms of healing were based on this understanding, and there was a well-recognized link between the energy of the individual and the energy of nature, the creator or the divine. The word chakra means literally "wheel" in Sanskrit, and it is symbolized as a spinning wheel of light through which prana – the life-force – moves. It is this life-force that forms the basis of the energy plan that unfolds in the following eight chapters.

Chakras and the West

Unfortunately for the developed world, knowledge about chakras and energy has been largely forgotten. Instead it has been replaced by a materialistic view of the world and a corresponding loss of spirituality. Alongside this has been an increase in people's general dissatisfaction with life. Yet the energy principle remains the foundation of eastern thinking. In Chinese traditional medicine, for example, the principle of chi is central. Chi (ki in Japanese) is the invisible life-force or energy that moves around the body freely when we are well. When there is an obstruction or a weak flow of this life-force, we become ill on a physical, emotional or spiritual level. Ancient Chinese exercise systems, such as tai chi and chi gong, are designed to promote the flow of chi around the body. Although, in the past, chi-based therapies, such as acupuncture, have been dismissed as a nonsense in the West, they are now increasingly accepted, and often used side-by-side with conventional western medical techniques.

The delay in the acceptance of eastern principles is largely owing to the way in which western medicine operates. We like to see how things work, whether it is the functioning of an organ in the body or a new drug that has been tested in the laboratory, using a placebo to guarantee that the effect is purely physical and not manipulated by the mind. The eastern approach to healing is very different: there is little you can see; and the mind is seen as an equal partner to the body, both as a cause of problems and as a solution to them.

Harnessing the Intangible

Chakras and energy have long played a crucial role in the Buddhist, Hindu and yogic understanding of how the body, mind and spirit interact. From these ancient eastern perspectives, bringing the chakras to their full potential and into balance with each other is seen as essential for both physical health and spiritual enlightenment. Yet, understanding – even accepting the existence of – the chakras can pose a challenge for the western mind, because the chakras are not usually visible to the eye (although there are people who are believed to be able to see chakras, as well as the auras that are closely linked to them).

One way of understanding the chakras from a western viewpoint is to see them as a symbolic way to understand our minds, bodies and spirits.

The Seven Chakras

There are seven major chakras (see page 11) and each one represents an important centre of the body's and the mind's energy, as well as a different stage of spiritual development. Each chakra embodies a different understanding of the human condition and has a different contribution to make to it. The chakras can be seen to represent not only the energetic core of our beings but also the many levels of our unique make-up and approach to life. It is when the chakras are open and receptive, and energy is free to travel between them, that we feel most at peace, grounded and balanced in life, and healthy in mind and body.

The chakras are aligned from root to crown as a column of energy and they are both conduits and generators of energy. Prana, or life-force, flows through the chakras and the rest of the body along a network of channels known as nadis. There are tens of thousands of nadis, but the most important one is the sushumna nadi, which starts at the root chakra and rises to the crown of the head. At its base – at the root chakra – lies a type of energy known as kundalini, which is symbolized by a sleeping serpent. One of the aims of yoga is to awaken this serpent and raise its energy up through the sushumna nadi

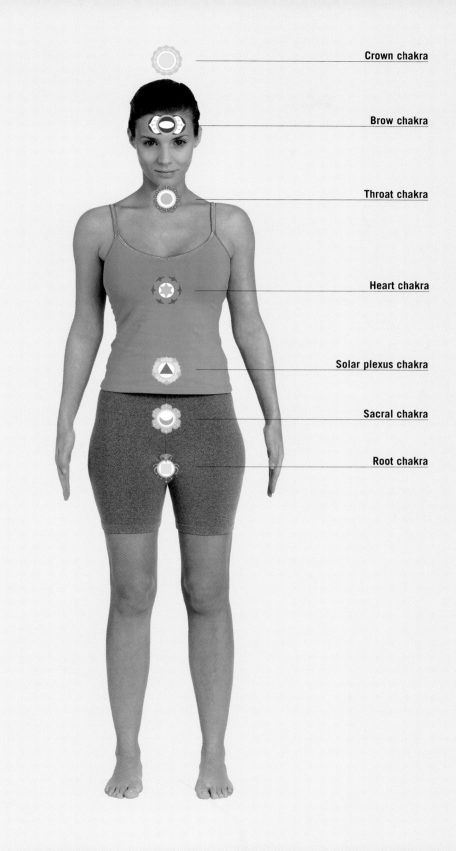

Crown chakra

Brow chakra

Throat chakra

Heart chakra

Solar plexus chakra

Sacral chakra

Root chakra

to the crown chakra. When kundalini energy reaches the crown chakra, we achieve a state of bliss and enlightenment.

Kundalini energy and the sushumna follow, in fact, much the same path as the spinal cord, but this path is within what is known as the subtle body (as opposed to the physical body). Each of the seven principal chakras lies along the sushumna, and each deals with its own concerns, but is inextricably linked to the next chakra, like a rung on a ladder. It is by ascending this ladder that we can travel from the realm of the individual and personal to the universal and spiritual. Yet it is wrong to think that higher chakras are more important than lower ones: all the chakras are of equal importance. In the same way that the body, the emotions and the mind are all interdependent and equally important, so are the chakras.

Opening the Chakras

When prana flows freely through the body, the chakras spin brighter and faster, and the body and mind are in a state of health. When there are blockages, or chakras are closed down altogether, prana cannot flow and "dis-ease" of the body, mind or spirit is the result. There are numerous causes for these blockages and closures – many of them easy to comprehend. For example, a child brought up without affection and the benefit of loving touch, may have difficulty as an adult opening the heart chakra. This not only holds him back from touching or showing affection, but also leaves him or her afraid of change, blocked creatively, and prone to a depressed immune system and, therefore, illness.

Chakra energy work is holistic: it involves the body and mind equally, because they are equally involved in our beings. The chakras are also linked closely to the endocrine system, which produces the hormones that act as chemical messengers – from adrenalin (epinephrine), which drives our "fight-or-flight" response, to the sex hormones, oestrogen and testosterone. When you balance your chakras, you also regulate your hormones.

Accessing the Power of the Universe

With chakra work you don't have only your own resources to draw upon: the chakras work with energy beyond the self as well as energy within the body. This energy may come via the root chakra's link to the earth's energy or via the crown chakra's relationship with universal, spiritual energy. Just as you are aiming for a sense of peace and harmony with the universe, the universe's energy is ready to support you – all you have to do is recognize this.

By working to open up our chakras, we also open up our possibilities in life. We not only improve our physical health, but we achieve a sense of emotional wholeness, a deeper connection with those around us and a sense of harmony with the world and our part and purpose in it.

Chakra Names and Correspondences

Name	Root	Sacral	Solar Plexus
Sanskrit Name	Muladhara (root)	Swadhisthana (sweetness)	Manipura (jewel city)
Drive	Survival	Sexuality	Willpower
Colour	Red	Orange	Yellow
Physical Body	Bones, teeth, legs, feet	Sex organs, bladder, kidneys, bodily fluids	Abdomen, digestive system, lower and middle back
Element	Earth	Water	Fire
Sense	Smell	Taste	Sight
Lotus Flower	Four red petals	Six orange petals	Ten yellow petals
Crystals	Tiger's eye, agate, bloodstone	Golden topaz, amber, citrine	Yellow citrine, fool's gold, topaz
Oils and Fragrances	Cedarwood, patchouli, myrrh	Musk, sandalwood	Bergamot, ylang-ylang
Animal	Elephant	Crocodile	Ram
Astrology – Planetary Affinities	Saturn	Pluto	Sun and Mars

Heart	Throat	Brow	Crown
Anahara (unstruck sound)	Vishuddha (purification)	Ajna (to perceive, to know)	Sahasrara (thousandfold)
Love	Communication	Inspiration	Transcendence
Green or pink	Blue	Indigo	Violet, gold or white
Heart, lungs, chest, upper back	Neck, throat, vocal chords	Face, eyes	Skull, brain, skin
Air	Ether	Light	Thought
Touch	Hearing	Intuition	Higher self
Twelve green or blue petals	Sixteen pale blue petals	Two white petals	One thousand golden petals
Rose quartz, watermelon tourmaline, jade	Lapis lazuli, turquoise, sodalite	Lapis lazuli, amethyst, fluorite	Clear quartz, diamond, white tourmaline
Rose, bergamot, neroli	Hyacinth, lavender	Violet, rose geranium	Frankincense, amber, lavender
Antelope	Elephant	None	None
Venus	Mercury	Neptune and Jupiter	Uranus

How to Use this Book

This is, above all, a practical book. Even though it deals with something quite intangible – energy – it aims to harness that energy in accessible and practical ways. The overall aim is to bring your physical, emotional, mental and spiritual energies into balance. This will enable you to live your life in a more positive way on every level.

This book offers a series of exercises that are designed to bring your energies into balance. It is important to remember that your different energies – physical, emotional, mental and spiritual – are inextricably entwined, and that one type of exercise or activity may affect you in a number of different ways. For example, yoga exercises may feel primarily physical, but as well as affecting your body they also act on your breath and your mind, bringing you more easily into a meditative state. And, while meditation may seem to be something that involves only your mind, it also brings about a profound relaxation of your body.

Each chapter of this book is devoted to one chakra, except for the last chapter, which is about balancing all of the chakras. While you may feel that you would like to work on one specific chakra (the heart and the brow are two common favourites), it is important to work on all of the chakras equally. Start with the root chakra before you move systematically up through each of the other chakras. Progressing in this way will provide an indication of which chakras need most work. This method will also help to keep your energy more balanced than if you focus on a single chakra. When you reach the crown chakra, start again at the beginning with the root chakra, so that you are working in a continuous cycle.

Yoga and Chi Gong Exercises
When you practise the yoga and chi gong exercises in this book, make sure that you have enough space to move freely, and wear loose, comfortable clothes. Turn off

phones and ensure that you won't be disturbed. When you are doing yoga exercises, work on a carpet or a yoga mat to prevent you slipping. Try to make enough time in your yoga practice to start with Salute to the Sun (see pages 132–3). At least once a week, do a longer yoga session, combining poses for each of the chakras.

Meditation and Visualization Exercises

Whether you are seated or lying on the floor, you need to have a straight spine for all of the meditation and breathing exercises. This is essential for the flow of energy between the chakras. If you are supple and you have a strong back, you can sit cross-legged or in full- or half-lotus position (see page 119). If not, make sure your back is supported, either by sitting against a wall, or in a chair in which your feet are flat on the floor. Keep a blanket to hand, as your temperature will drop slightly during meditation.

You may want to record the guided meditations at the end of each chapter. It is a lot easier to listen to a recording than to try to remember all the steps. When you are recording, speak slowly, calmly and without modulation – this helps the mind to focus. Leave long pauses so that you can do each step without being rushed.

Finally, don't expect to be able to meditate instantly. Thoughts will intrude and you might even fall asleep. Don't worry about this. When you realize your mind has wandered, just let the thoughts go and bring the mind back to its focus without making any judgment or feeling frustrated. It may help to see the thoughts as clouds or wisps of smoke floating away from you.

The Root Chakra

Muladhara

The root chakra is the first in the column of chakras. Our most basic instinct — for survival — lies within this chakra, as do our needs for food, sleep and shelter. The root chakra is the base of powerful kundalini energy, which rises through all the chakras to reach the crown, where it brings about the meditative state of samadhi.

As part of the survival instinct, the root chakra is closely linked with security, emotional as well as physical. When it is out of balance, you may suffer from low self-esteem, feel out of touch with your body and your sexuality, or be prone to depression and addictive behaviour, such as smoking. When your root chakra is balanced, you feel confident and healthy, and happy with your body and your sexuality.

About the Root Chakra

The root chakra, represented by a lotus flower with four red petals, is governed by the element of earth, which gives it a grounded "earthy" quality. Until your root chakra is balanced, enabling you to feel safe and in touch with your body, spiritual development is impossible.

The root chakra grounds you in your body and gives you a feeling of safety. It is strongly linked to the crown chakra and, between them, they govern the body's hormone system. Without a balanced root chakra, the crown cannot function.

The root chakra's element is earth. It reaches down the legs to the foot chakras (see page 28) to draw up the earth's energy. When you sit on the ground to meditate, the root chakra – which lies between the genitals and anus on the perineum – is in direct contact with earth energy.

In an emergency you need to marshall all your physical resources, and the root chakra enables you to do this. The glands associated with this chakra are the adrenal glands, which produce the hormone adrenalin (epinephrine) as part of the fight-or-flight response. Adrenalin gives you extra strength and stamina in a crisis, allowing you to run away from attack, for example.

Your early years have a profound influence on the health of your root chakra. It is thought that babies who are fed on demand and given plenty of love and security are much more likely to have healthy root chakras. Those deprived of love or left to cry when hungry tend to become needy and prone to developing a victim mentality. A closed root chakra in adulthood may mean that you constantly worry about money or never feel satisfied with your work or home. It can also lead to self-destructive or addictive behaviour – such as eating disorders, smoking, drug-taking, drinking too much alcohol, or gambling – or to illnesses, such as lower back pain, hemorrhoids, constipation and sciatica. Depression may result from a dislike of your own body. On the other hand, a root chakra that is too open can lead to isolation; materialism; selfish, bullying behaviour; or an addiction to loveless sexuality.

A balanced root chakra makes you feel physically secure, able to be part of a group without being domineering or needy, and confident to trust your instincts and follow your destiny. A strong, firm massage can stabilize the root chakra. You can also nourish it with a balanced diet and plenty of sleep. Your root chakra thrives on physical challenge, so participating in sport is a good way to stimulate this chakra. Specific smells (see page 30) can both stimulate and calm the root chakra.

Yoga to Ground Your Body

The root chakra is the grounding chakra, the one that connects you to the earth and your own physicality. The following yoga postures all have a centring and settling effect. You can practise them by themselves or as a preliminary sequence to the other yoga postures in this book. Grounding exercises are fundamental to all chakra work.

Mountain Pose

It looks as if very little is happening in Mountain Pose, or Tadasana – after all, you're just standing still! As you will discover, there is a good deal more to the posture than this. Stand in Mountain Pose and take time to observe your breathing. This will centre you both physically and mentally. This posture, and the next, both engage the mula bandha (see page 28). Treat Mountain Pose as a preliminary to all other yoga postures.

Stand, preferably in front of a mirror, with your feet hip-width apart, toes pointing straight forward and arms at your sides. Look straight ahead so that you gaze into your own eyes. Make sure that there is no tension in your shoulders, back or neck. Breathe in and with your arms slightly away from your body, stretch them and point your fingers down toward the ground. Don't let any tension creep into your shoulders or neck. Breathe out and pull your navel back and up toward your spine. Lift your ribs and open and soften your chest. Breathe slowly and deeply for five breaths.

Fierce Posture

This posture, known in Sanskrit as Utkasana, follows on naturally from Mountain Pose. It is grounding in the same way, but has a much stronger effect. Take care not to let your shoulders or neck become tense as you reach upward.

From Mountain Pose, breathe in and, as you breathe out, bend your knees without letting your heels come off the ground. Keep your navel pulled up and back toward your spine. On your next out-breath, raise your arms above your head and place your palms together in prayer position. Don't lift your shoulders. Look up toward your fingers. Breathe slowly and deeply for five breaths. If your back aches in this pose, you are probably not fully engaging the bandhas (see page 28). In particular, your abdominal muscles may not be strong enough and you may need to work more on strengthening uddiyana bandha (see page 54). If your shoulders or neck feel tense in this pose, try doing it with your hands apart, palms facing and fingers stretched to the ceiling. If you have neck problems, look straight ahead rather than upward.

Forward Bends

This cycle of poses, called Paschimothanasana, establishes the link between the root and crown chakras that runs the length of the spine. This is one of the most important chakra connections and it promotes a strong flow of energy. Forward Bends also calm and settle the mind and improve posture and suppleness. Learning how to bend in these postures is of supreme importance. Most people automatically bend the spine when they bend forward. In these postures you should bend, not from your spine, but from your hips, like a hinge. The aim is not to hunch over as low as you can, but to make your spine into a long energized line.

1 Sit on the floor with your legs straight out in front of you and your back straight. Relax your shoulders and sit up high on your "sitting bones". Don't slump. Your whole body should feel lifted without tension. Make sure that your neck is in line with your spine. Flex your heels so that the backs of your knees are – as much as possible – on the floor.

2 Breathe in and, as you breathe out, bend forward from your hips without rounding your spine. Keep your neck in line with your spine. Concentrate not on how low you can get, but on how long and stretched. On your next out-breath, hold your ankles or calves (depending on how flexible you are) and use your hands as a lever to help pull you down further. Keep your spine long and straight. When you have reached the full extent of your stretch, take five long, slow breaths, each time trying to relax and reach further into the posture.

Deepening the Stretch

In time you will become more supple and able to deepen the stretches on the previous page. These hand positions will help you. Be careful not to strain – if something feels uncomfortable, stop.

1 Wrap your hands around your feet. You can hold the soles of your feet from the sides or over the tops of your toes. Try both variations as they will give a slightly different stretch.

2 Before you stretch forward, place your hands in prayer position behind your back. Let your fingers get as high up toward the shoulders as they will reach, but don't allow any tension to creep into your shoulders. Breathe in and, as you breathe out, bend forward from your hips over your legs.

Chi Gong to Root Your Body

As with the yoga postures, the chi gong movements for the root chakra ground and connect you with the earth. The Basic Stance in every form of tai chi and chi gong is the most fundamental of all the positions.

Basic Stance

Like the Mountain Pose (see page 22) in yoga, Basic Stance looks simple, but there is more going on in the posture than first appears. Concentrate on allowing your weight to sink as you bend your knees.

Stand with your feet shoulder-width apart and your weight evenly distributed over both feet. Bend your knees and feel your spine drop in a long straight line toward the ground. Iron out any exaggerated curve in your lower back by slightly tilting your pelvis. Check that there is no tension in your neck, and that your shoulders are relaxed rather than raised. Your arms should be a little way away from your body. Try to sense your connection with the earth through the soles of your feet. Let your weight be centred in your lower body.

SIDE VIEW

Rooting to the Earth

This exercise teaches you the correct way to shift your weight in tai chi and chi gong. Keep the turns slow and smooth.

1 Lift your arms to chest height and round them, as if you are holding a large beach ball. Without straightening your knees, shift your body to the right so that your right foot takes your weight (lift your left foot to check). Now, smoothly transfer your weight onto your left foot. Transfer your weight from side to side slowly four times, feeling the weight dropping down into the ground.

2 When your weight is over to the left, rotate your left foot and your body in a smooth movement to face left. Visualize your spine as a pole around which you are moving. Don't straighten your left knee. Still facing left, let your weight settle evenly between both feet. Now rotate to face right. Transfer your weight onto your right foot. Repeat this turning movement from side to side four times.

Balancing the Root Chakra

You can balance your root chakra in a number of ways: by giving yourself a relaxing foot massage or visiting a massage therapist or reflexologist; by employing a muscular lock known as mula bandha during yoga practice; and by paying attention to your surroundings. You can also nurture your root chakra using essential oils or incense.

A foot massage is a relaxing way to balance the root chakra. As well as the seven main chakras, there are secondary chakras that are connected with them. In the centre of the arches of your feet are chakras that are linked with your root chakra. These provide the link between your own energy and the earth's cleansing energy. Walking barefoot on grass or sand stimulates the foot chakras. The grounding and earthing work for the root chakra in the yoga and chi gong exercises on pages 20–27 is another way of opening up these foot chakras.

The foot massage opposite is easy to do by yourself. It incorporates some reflexology techniques, which, as well as being relaxing, will have the beneficial effect of stimulating the circulation of blood and lymph around your body. The main underlying principle of reflexology is that there are reflex points on the feet that correspond to every organ and part of the body. By treating the feet you are effectively treating the whole person. You should not practise this foot massage if you have varicose veins or a heart condition, or if you are pregnant.

The Root Lock

There are three locks or "bandhas" that are used in yoga. They promote the flow of both prana (life-force) and kundalini energy. They are: mula bandha, uddiyana bandha (see page 54) and jalandhara bandha (see page 94). Mula bandha is an intrinsic part of the root chakra. It shares its name base with the Sanskrit name of the chakra: Muladhara. One of the reasons yoga is so important for the health of the chakras is that it encourages the flow of prana around the body generally and, in particular, through the central sushumna channel (see page 10).

The mula bandha is engaged by lifting the perineum upward into the body. The mula bandha should be engaged in many of the yoga exercises throughout this book. It can be strongly engaged or weakly engaged, depending on how strong your muscles are in this area. Men and women will experience the sensation of lifting mula bandha differently owing to their different arrangement of muscles in the perineum.

At first it may be difficult to isolate the muscles of the perineum from the anal

MASSAGING YOUR FEET

Wear loose, comfortable clothes and sit with your back supported. You will need to find the best position to access the sole of each foot. This may be cross-legged, or on a chair with your foot resting on the thigh of the opposite leg. If you wish, you can apply a light moisturizer before the massage. Use a firm touch throughout. Wear cotton socks before and after the massage to keep your feet warm.

1 Start by relaxing your foot. Hold your foot so that one hand is on the sole and one on the top. Working from your ankle to your toes, massage it with long, firm strokes on both top and bottom.

2 Holding your heel in one hand and your toes in the other, circle your foot around your ankle five times clockwise and anticlockwise.

3 Starting with your big toe, stroke the top and bottom of each toe in turn and, when your reach the tip, gently pull the toe to stretch it out. Repeat this three times.

4 Using your thumb and starting at your big toe, move along the line of pads just below your toes. Press each one firmly before moving on to the next. Work your way to your little toe, then change hands, and using your other thumb, work your way back. Repeat this twice.

5 Use your thumb to press down gently from the top to the base of the underside of your big toe. Repeat on all of your toes. When you reach your little toe, change hands and use the other thumb to go back the other way. Repeat twice.

6 Holding your toes in one hand, use the thumb of your other hand to press along the sole. Press in a line from the base of your big toe to the centre of your foot, following the line of the metatarsal bone. Repeat on all your toes, then repeat on the top of your foot, following the same line.

7 Starting at your heel, use your thumb to press along the inside edge of your foot all the way up to your big toe. Press firmly and follow the line up over your instep. Then repeat on the outside edge of your foot, from your heel to your little toe.

8 Finally, massage the lower half of your sole, using firm pressure. Rotate your foot around your ankle, both clockwise and anticlockwise. Repeat step 1 using long, firm strokes from your ankle to your toes. Put on a cotton sock and repeat the massage on the other foot.

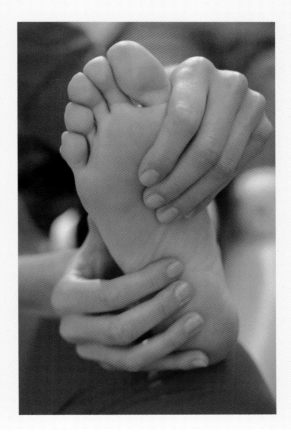

sphincter muscle but, with practice, you can learn to dissociate them. The following pelvic floor exercises will help to you locate and engage the perineum. It is a good idea, incidentally, for all women to practise pelvic floor exercises, particularly during pregnancy and after giving birth. When you fisrt do them, you may find that you can contract your muscles only very briefly before the contraction seems to slip away. You can do pelvic floor exercises at any time and in any place – including in public – as outwardly, it looks as though you are doing nothing at all!

Pelvic Floor Exercises

If you're not sure where your pelvic floor muscles are, the easiest way to locate them is to stop and start your flow of urine in midstream. The muscles that you contract and relax in order to do this are your pelvic floor muscles. Once you have identified the right muscles, you are ready to start pelvic floor exercises.

1. Slowly contract your pelvic floor muscles in a long, upward movement. Your body should not move outwardly as you do this, and your abdomen and buttocks should remain relaxed. Hold the contrac-

YOUR SENSE OF SMELL

The sense that is associated with the root chakra is smell. Smell is the first sense that we become aware of as babies. The most important first smell is that of the mother and her milk. (Coincidentally, the term used to describe a baby's search for the nipple is rooting.) Smell is also, perhaps, **the most evocative of the senses. A particular smell can revive a stream of memories. For me, the scent of chrysanthemums is forever related to cemeteries. It will always summon up the image of putting flowers on my grandparents' grave as a very young child.**

You can balance the root chakra through your sense of smell by using incense or essential oils. If you are using essential oils, you can put a few drops in a bath and relax there for about 20 minutes or you can use them, as you would incense, in a ring burner over a lamp to scent the air. Lavender is a very balancing fragrance and you can use it in a diffuser to permeate a room or your whole house. You can also add it to body oils or lotions or put a few drops on your pillow to induce a deep, restful sleep – something which is very nourishing for the root chakra. Cedar is a lovely open-air smell that is soothing for the root chakra (you can buy cedar-scented joss sticks). You can also use fresh flowers – one of the most stimulating smells for the root chakra comes from a bowl of spring hyacinths.

Your sense of smell is closely related to your sense of taste and your enjoyment of food. Just imagine the delightful aroma of freshlymade coffee or newly-baked bread – it's the smell and the taste combined that make them so appealing. To truly nourish the root chakra you should eat not only nutritiously but also with pleasure. This means taking time over choosing food, and preparing and cooking it in a mindful way. When you sit down to eat, don't rush to put the food in your mouth. Take a moment to close your eyes and savour the smells rising from your plate. Indulge in ripe fruits full of scent and flavour as well as a delicious taste. Revel in the physicality and sensuality of food. To paraphrase T.S. Eliot in *The Love Song of J. Alfred Prufrock* – do you dare to eat a peach?

tion and then slowly release it. Repeat this 10 times.

2. Repeat step one but this time imagine that your muscles are a lift that is going to stop at five floors. Stop at each floor and hold the contraction before going on to the next. Hold the contraction at the top and then repeat, stage by stage, on the way down.

Creating the Right Environment

Satisfaction with your environment is important for balancing the root chakra. Shelter is an intrinsic part of the root chakra's will to survive and this applies both to your individual home and your wider environment. The colour of the root chakra is red and you can nurture this chakra by bringing this colour into your home. If you're thinking of painting the walls, use a dark rose-pink or earthy terracotta. These colours work brilliantly in rooms that you want to warm up or ones that you use for particular functions, such as studying or dining. I have three north-facing rooms in variations of these shades and the colour compensates for the lack of direct sunlight. If you like crimsons and scarlets, try to use them in moderation, as accent colours in rugs, cushions or pillows – if they cover too wide an area, they are unsettling for the other chakras.

A wider and perhaps more difficult question in terms of environment is whether you are in the right geographical setting. You may be happy and successful in your work, but perhaps it ties you to a city when your root chakra's earthy nature (and many other elements in your essential make-up) is tugging you toward the country, the sea or the mountains. On the other hand, you may be a city kid at heart and yet stuck out in the wilds. Moving may not even be a remote possibility, but being in wrong place can throw you off kilter. If you yearn for the woods or the ocean, try to visit as often as you can. Being in nature restores not just the earthy root chakra, but the higher spiritual chakras, which thrive on the contemplation of beauty.

Chakra Work and Crystals

Crystal work can balance your root chakra – for more information on how to use crystals, see pages 124–5. Crystals that reflect the root chakra's reds and browns are useful: try bloodstone, tiger's eye or fire agate. It can be particularly useful to meditate with crystals to solve the practical problems – perhaps involving money or work – that the root chakra throws up. Sit in a chair with your back supported and place a crystal on top of each foot in line with the foot chakras (see page 28). Close your eyes and settle your mind by focusing on a few deep breaths. Then focus on the problem or question you have – whether it is to do with money, health, self-belief or anything else. Don't try to find a solution, just look at the problem and recognize that you are strong enough to deal with it. Feel the crystals drawing the earth's energy up through your foot chakras and into your body, infusing you with newfound strength. Be aware that there is a higher energy that can help you. Ask that higher energy for help.

Root Chakra Meditation

The root chakra has a special energy, known in Sanskrit as kundalini. This is an extremely powerful force and, when it is liberated, it runs straight up through the body and all of the chakras, connecting finally with the crown chakra at the top of the head.

The chakras lie within a vertical column, known as the sushumna, roughly equivalent in location to the spinal cord. Kundalini is also the name of the Hindu serpent goddess and kundalini energy is often portrayed as a snake rising from the root chakra, piercing and awakening each chakra in turn as it spirals around the sushumna on its way to the crown.

In the Buddhist tradition – which, incidentally, has only five chakras – pure mental energy can flow up sushumna only when this channel is free from negative feelings. If feelings, such as anger or jealousy, centre themselves on the chakras, energy gets diverted into two channels that run to the left and right of the central channel. As a result, energy cannot reach and cleanse the chakras and, ultimately, move up to the crown chakra.

The inner heat meditation on the opposite page helps to cleanse your energy allowing it to flow freely so that you can meditate on a pure state of bliss without worldly attachments.

This is a very powerful meditation when done in its entirety. The first time you do it, draw the heated energy up only as far as the heart chakra. Work up to the higher chakras over a long period of time. If you do feel a sudden kundalini rush that leaves you dizzy or overwhelmed, bring your focus back to your breath, slowing it down until your mind is calm.

INNER HEAT MEDITATION

This meditation can produce feelings of deep peace and serenity that flow through your body and mind. Enjoy this feeling for as long as possible. It is a good idea to read the meditation a few times before you try it so that you have a clear idea of the positions of the three main energy channels in your body. Try to hold these channels in your mind's eye as you do the meditation. Aim to get a strong sense of the cleansing heat of the fire. Inner heat meditation is a useful practice at times when you are feeling troubled or blocked by negative thoughts – afterward you will feel as though all your troubles have been burned away.

Sit in a comfortable position with a straight back. Spend a few moments composing yourself, settling your mind and concentrating on your breath. Close your eyes and take three long, deep breaths. Focus on the breath entering your body and filling your lungs and cells with life-giving oxygen. As you exhale imagine that you are breathing out any negative thoughts that are holding you back.

Breathe normally again as you visualize the three energy channels that run along the midline of your body – the central sushumna channel and the two smaller channels on either side of it. The central channel is parallel to the spinal column and reaches all the way up to the crown of your head from the base of your spine. The narrower side channels begin at your nostrils and loop over the crown of your head and down the sides of the central channel where they join it close to the sacral chakra. All of the channels are hollow, waiting to be filled with energy.

Picture a tiny piece of glowing charcoal and mentally place it inside the central channel at the solar plexus chakra. You can feel that it is warm, but you need to increase its heat by slowly engaging the mula bandha (see page 28), drawing up energy from the root chakra to fan the flames.

Breathe in so that the air flows down the side channels to where they join the central one at the sacral chakra, just below the charcoal, stoking the fire still more. Now, holding your breath, pull your rib cage in so that the air is trapped by both the rib cage and the mula bandha. Watch the heat increase in the charcoal. Slowly breathe out, relax all your muscles and visualize the heated, cleansed energy rising up the central channel toward the crown chakra. Repeat three times, building up to seven over a period of time. On the last inhalation, imagine the charcoal bursting into flames that shoot up the central channel. The flames destroy negative feelings, cleanse each chakra and open the crown chakra to pure energy that flows down the central channel to the fire.

Slowly bring your focus back to your breath and then gradually become aware of your physical body. Rest for a few moments before slowly opening your eyes.

The Sacral Chakra

Swadhisthana

Swadhisthana is Sanskrit for "sweetness". The sacral chakra is the seat of pleasure, and of taste in its broadest sense — not just food, but clothes, music, design and colour. It is all about attraction and, in particular, sexuality (sexual identity and pleasure rather than the primal sexuality of the root chakra). The sacral chakra is also the centre for our emotions.

The sacral chakra is the most feminine of the seven chakras. It is profoundly connected with fertility and is ruled by the moon, which pulls not only the seas and oceans, but the waters within our own bodies. A balanced sacral chakra is often characterized by physical fluidity and grace.

About the Sacral Chakra

The sacral chakra is represented by a lotus with six orange petals surrounding a white circle – which indicates water – and a light blue crescent moon. The sacral chakra governs bodily fluids, emotions and sexuality. They ebb and flow, drawn like tides by the moon.

The sacral chakra is situated in the lower abdomen between your navel and genitals. It governs your spleen, reproductive organs (testes or ovaries), kidneys and bladder, and all your bodily fluids, including blood, saliva, seminal fluid, and lymph. Our bodies are mostly fluid – we're about 75 per cent water – and water therapies are the most effective way of balancing the sacral chakra.

Good sacral-chakra balance is characterized by physical grace, whereas lack of balance results in physical awkwardness or lack of co-ordination. Teenage boys, coming to terms with their emotions and sexuality, typically have unbalanced sacral chakras.

As well as being graceful, people with a balanced sacral chakra tend to be friendly, open and trusting, in touch with their feelings and able to express them, willing to see the positive rather than the negative, and able to turn problems into challenges. An out-of-balance sacral chakra brings about guilt, self-pity, manipulative behaviour and envy. If your sacral chakra is too open, you may forget your own needs, and occupy yourself so much with the needs of others that you end up feeling like a martyr. Lack of balance in the sacral chakra can also give rise to sexual problems, jealousy and obsession – sexuality is at the heart of the sacral chakra.

It is sexual awareness – rather than primal sex drive – that characterizes the sacral chakra. It guides our sexual identity, our ability to bond with a partner and to take pleasure in our sexuality. When in balance, the sacral chakra can give us profound sexual and emotional happiness. When out of balance, all kinds of problems can arise. If you have a closed or blocked sacral chakra, you can become obsessed with sex or your own sexuality, and have total disregard for partners. You may see sex as a purely physical, hedonistic act, devoid of emotion. At the other extreme you may become frigid or impotent. Sexual abuse is a common cause of a closed second chakra. It is worth reflecting, perhaps, that the word "sacral" comes from the same root as "sacred". Sex is not meant to be a casual, meaningless event, but nor is it meant to induce guilt. Rather, with openness and empathy, it is something that brings great joy and pleasure.

Yoga to Stimulate the Sacral Chakra

These yoga postures stimulate the internal organs associated with the sacral chakra, such as the kidneys and bladder. They also stimulate the circulation of blood and lymph. Some of the postures, notably Tailor Pose, work on the reproductive organs and can help to relieve problems such as menstrual cramp.

Cow Face

Even though Cow Face, or Gomukasana in Sanskrit, looks like a closed and twisted pose, it is a great way of opening up and releasing tension from your sacral area and your upper back and shoulders.

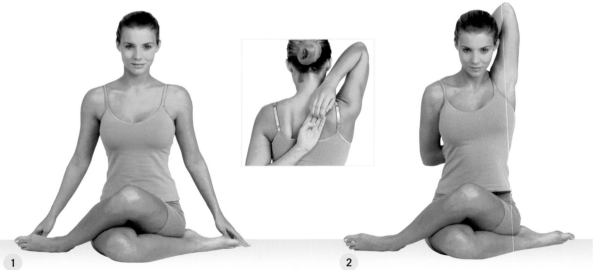

1 Sit on the floor with your back straight and your legs out in front of you. Bend your right leg under the left, with your right foot close to your left hip. Now bend your left leg so that your left knee is on top of your right knee.

2 Take your left arm over your head, bending the elbow so that your fingers reach down your back. Bend your right arm behind your back so that your fingers reach toward those of your left hand. Clasp your fingers if you can. If you can't, use a belt or a scarf to bridge the gap. Take five long, slow breaths and then repeat on the other side of your body.

Warrior Pose

This pose, known in Sanskrit as Virabhadrasana, is a strong posture that works on your pelvis, hips and lower back. Two variations are shown here. Try to keep both postures solid and centred. Don't overextend your knees or allow your body to become twisted – this may damage your back or knees.

1 Stand with your feet about 1.2 m (4 ft) apart with your feet parallel and your toes facing straight ahead. Breathe in and, as you breathe out, lift your arms straight up at the sides to shoulder height, palms facing downward. Stretch out your arms all the way to your fingertips. Don't let your shoulders become tense.

2 Turn your left foot out to a 90-degree angle and slightly turn in your right foot. Breathe in and, as you breathe out, draw your navel to your spine and engage the mula and uddiyana bandhas (see pages 28 and 54). At the same time bend your left knee to a right angle. Keep your hips open and your arms stretched, and turn your head to look out over your left arm. This is the first variation of Warrior Pose. Take five long, deep breaths. Straighten your left leg, return to the centre and repeat on the other side of your body.

3 To do the second variation of Warrior Pose, begin with step 1, but, when you turn your feet in step 2, turn your hips, too, so that you are facing your left leg. Breathe in and, without lifting or tensing your shoulders, raise your arms above your head. Breathe out, engaging the mula and uddiyana bandhas, and bend your left knee to a right angle. Keep your spine long and straight (don't strain your lower back). Place your palms together in prayer position and look up toward them. Take five long, deep breaths. Repeat on the other side of your body.

Tailor Pose

The aim of Tailor Pose, or Baddha Konasana, is to hinge forward at your hips with a long straight spine. Avoid bending from your waist, rounding your back or hunching your shoulders in an attempt to get closer to the floor – it is more important to do the posture correctly.

1 Sit on the floor with the soles of your feet together and your back straight and free from tension. If you find this difficult, sit on a thick book or a very firm cushion. Engage the mula and uddiyana bandhas (see page 28 and 54), place your hands on your ankles or calves, and take five deep breaths.

2 Try to drop your knees further toward the floor by allowing your hip joints to relax and open. Take five, long deep breaths. On your last out-breath, bend forward from your hips with a long, straight back. Try to keep your hip joints as open as possible and don't let your shoulders become tense. Take five long, deep breaths and return to the sitting position that you started in.

Side Stretch

This is a lovely open stretch that massages the sacral chakra's internal organs. Make sure that you work hard enough to feel the stretch, but not so hard that you strain yourself.

1 Sit with your legs stretched as wide apart as is comfortable. Keep your back straight and your neck in line with your spine. Breathe in and engage the mula and uddiyana bandhas. Your knees should face the ceiling – don't let them roll inward. Flex your feet so that your toes point upward. Breathe in and raise your arms to shoulder height with your palms facing up. Keeping your shoulders and neck relaxed.

2 As you breathe out stretch to the side and down toward your right leg. Keep your chest facing forward. Use your right hand to hold your leg and help to lever your body down. Don't let any tension creep into your shoulders or neck. Keep both buttocks on the floor.

3 On your next out-breath, lift your left arm to reach over your head, keeping it in line with your body. Turn to face your left arm and take five long, deep breaths. Repeat on the other side of your body.

Chi Gong to Stimulate the Sacral Chakra

This exercise, known as Rowing the Boat, combines a forward bend with arm rotations. Make all of your movements graceful, fluid and seamless.

Rowing the Boat
This sequence of movements is good for your back and your kidney area.

1 Begin in the Basic Stance (see page 26) and turn your attention inward by taking some long, deep breaths. Check your posture, drop your shoulders and let go of any feelings of tension. Lower your eyes and let your gaze rest on the ground a short distance in front of you.

2 With your palms facing down, raise your arms in front of you at shoulder height.

3 Turn your palms to face upward and raise your arms until your fingers point to the ceiling. Keep your shoulders relaxed.

4 Slowly lower your arms in front of your body. As you bring your arms forward, bend your knees and lean forward with your fingers outstretched.

5 Keep your knees bent and fold forward from your waist. Drop your head toward the floor and reach your hands behind you in a wide, slow circle.

1   2   3   4   5

6 Let your arms reach as far as they can behind you and bring them overhead.

7 Keep moving your arms in a wide circle. As your arms are near to completing the circle, start to uncurl your body.

8 Uncurl into a fully upright position.

9 Lower your arms to the sides to start again. Repeat this movement ten times.

6   7   8   9

Balancing the Sacral Chakra

Water is essential to the health of the sacral chakra. Most people, these days, are dehydrated. Although few of us are likely die from lack of water, the vast majority of us are dehydrated to the point where our health is affected. Drinking more water will improve both your general health and the health of your sacral chakra. Hydrotherapy also balances the sacral chakra.

People have always been drawn to and refreshed by water. Being by water calms and energizes us. Being in water relaxes and strengthens us. Water is synonymous with purity, and its cleansing properties are not merely physical. All of the world's great religions use water symbolically for the purification of the soul. And at the dawn of prehistory, our ancestors often made their shrines at the point where a spring bubbled up from the ground. This denotes the important link between earth and water, and, correspondingly, the root and sacral chakras.

The water purification exercises on pages 46–7 are profoundly cleansing and relaxing. If you can, spend a whole day rehydrating (see page 47), and energizing and relaxing your sacral chakra. Start by doing the salt scrub (see box, opposite) and alternating showers (see pages 46–7). Go swimming or spend time near water. Try the meditation on page 49.

Why We Need Water

Water acts as the body's waste disposal system, getting rid of toxins and dead cells, particles of pollution (and any medications you are taking) and excreting them through your liver or kidneys, or as sweat. The lymphatic system – the prime mover in the immune system – also depends on water to keep its fluid (lymph) transporting water, protein, white blood cells, and electrolytes around the body. All of your other body systems also depend upon water in order to function.

Drink the Right Amount

Most people are not even aware of being dehydrated. Some of the signs include dry skin, dark urine and lack of concentration, but these usually occur before you even feel thirsty. In fact, feeling thirsty is not a reliable indicator of when to drink. Your body gets accustomed to however much water you give it, but what it needs is 2 litres (3.5 pints) a day; more if you are in a hot, dry climate or doing lots of exercise.

Drinking this amount of water daily will have a remarkable effect on your health. It will have an immediate effect on your kidneys (which can deteriorate without enough water to help process the body's toxins). An optimum intake of water improves the circulation of blood and

SALT BODY SCRUB

This is a wonderfully refreshing way to start the day. I have experienced a version where you are hosed down afterward with an icy jet of water (very popular in traditional European spas), but this is not absolutely necessary! Here, the aim is to slough off the dead skin cells and stimulate the circulation of both blood and lymph (this in turn stimulates your immune system and cell renewal). You can buy ready-made salt scrubs or you can make your own. For the latter use coarse rock salt in flakes and mix them into a paste with olive or sesame oil in a ratio of one handful of salt to one tablespoon of oil. To make the mixture smell nice, you can add a drop of an essential oil, such as rose or lavender.

Take care not to rub salt into any cuts or sores. Make sure that the bathroom is warm, with plenty of towels and a towelling robe ready for when you get out of the shower.

1 Stand under a warm shower for a minute or two until your whole body is wet. Step away from the water, take a handful of the scrub mixture and, starting with your feet, massage it well into your skin using circular movements with your whole hand. Make sure that you scrub the soles of your feet, too, and work on any hard or calloused skin that has built up.

2 Gradually work your way up your legs, using the same circular movements all the time. Pay particular attention to massaging your thighs and buttocks.

3 Reach those parts of your back that you are able to, and then very gently massage your abdomen in a circular clockwise direction, and then your chest or breasts.

4 Finally, scrub your arms and shoulders, as well as the hands themselves. Make sure that you move up your arms toward your shoulders, always in the direction of your heart.

5 Step back under the shower and carry on scrubbing the mixture into your skin as the water washes it off. Now try alternating showers (see pages 46–7).

enhances the function of your digestive and nervous systems. The quality and texture of your skin improves when you become properly hydrated, and you even become more energetic and mentally alert, and better able to concentrate.

Spend Time Near or In Water

Being close to the sea or a river will balance your sacral chakra. The simple act of walking ankle-deep in the sea along the shoreline, for example, not only puts you in contact with the water itself, but is also a deeply pleasurable experience – and pleasure is another important way of balancing the sacral chakra.

Swimming in the sea, a lake or a swimming pool is a perfect way to be in contact with water. Hydrotherapy (water therapy) or thalassotherapy (sea-water therapy) spas are also wonderful for the well-being of the sacral chakra. Even steam baths and jacuzzis are highly beneficial.

Alternating Showers

A simple hydrotherapy technique, known as alternating showers, stimulates your immune system, your nervous system and the circulation of blood and lymph.
1 Stand under a hot shower and let the water pour over you for two to three minutes, making sure that your whole body,

HERBAL TEA

You can vary your water intake by drinking herbal teas. There are lots of ready-made herbal teas available or you can make your own using a tea strainer and fresh herbs. Herbal teas shouldn't actually contain black tea (with its accompanying tannin and caffeine). If you are buying a ready-made herbal tea, check the list of ingredients to make sure that they do not include black tea. A more accurate name for herbal tea is an infusion or tisane. Not all so-called herbal teas contain herbs – some contain spices and fruit, and these are just as good. Fruit teas are sweet and refreshing; those with spices are stimulating. If you drink green or white tea, make sure that it is in addition to your 2-litre (3.5 pint) intake of water.

To make a herbal infusion at home, pour freshly boiled water onto your choice of herb/spice (there are some suggestions below) and leave it to steep for at least five minutes. If an infusion tastes bitter, add a teaspoon of organic honey.

Peppermint
Chop leaves finely and place in pot or cup, then cover with boiling water. Peppermint is a general pick-me-up and energizer.

Ginger
Chop a small chunk of root ginger into small pieces and leave to infuse for at least 10 minutes. Better still, make a flask and drink throughout the day – it gets stronger over time. Ginger stimulates blood and lymph circulation.

Camomile
Make in the same way as peppermint. Camomile is soothing for the nervous and digestive systems, as well as the emotions. It helps with anxiety, insomnia, cystitis, water retention, and bloating.

Cinnamon, Cloves and Nutmeg
Use cinnamon sticks, chopped nutmegs or a few cloves, either singly or together, and steep in a pot for at least 10 minutes. These spices all promote good circulation.

Lemon Balm
Make in the same way as peppermint tea. This soothing herb calms and lifts the spirits.

REHYDRATION PROGRAM

This rehydration program is one of the best things you can do for the health of your sacral chakra. It is important to remember that water by itself is the only drink that will properly rehydrate you. You should drink filtered (not softened) or bottled water. For variety, drink herbal tea (see box, opposite). Other drinks, such as tea, coffee, alcohol and fizzy drinks, either overload the body with sugar and caffeine or add to your dehydration – or both!

7am Your body loses water during the night, so drink a large glass (250ml/8fl oz) of water as soon as you wake up. This will also help to detoxify your kidneys and liver. Have your breakfast at least half an hour afterward.

9am If your means of transport to work is dry, hot, overcrowded or stressful, then your body will already have started to dehydrate. Drink from a bottle of water while you travel or drink your second glass of water now.

11am Drink a third glass of water; more if you find yourself in a hot or arid environment.

12.30pm Drink a glass of water half an hour before you have lunch.

2pm Drink your fifth glass of water to ensure clear thinking. At this time of day many people experience a dip in their concentration and energy levels.

4pm Instead of having an afternoon cup of tea or coffee, have a cup of herbal tea or drink your sixth glass of water.

6pm Drink another glass of water as you leave work or when you get home. Leave at least half an hour before you eat.

9pm Drink your last glass of water before you go to bed to prevent nighttime dehydration. However, don't drink water so close to your bedtime that it causes you to wake up during the night needing to go to the toilet.

including your head and face, is covered by the flow of water. If you want to wash using soap, shower gel or shampoo, do this now so that you can spend the rest of the time under pure water.

2 Turn the tap to cool or, if you're brave, cold (build up to this gradually) and let it cover your body for 15 to 30 seconds, or up to a minute when you get used to it.

3 Turn the water to hot for another two to three minutes, then back to cold. Alternate temperatures in this way up to three times and finish with hot water. Get out of the shower, wrap yourself in a warm towel and then put on a warm dressing gown. Lie down for half an hour. As you become accustomed to this technique, build up the overall length of time you spend in the shower, as well as the number of times you alternate the temperature.

Massage for the Sacral Chakra

A type of massage, known as manual lymphatic drainage (MLD), is a good way to balance the sacral chakra. As its name suggests, it stimulates the flow of lymph in the lymphatic system. MLD is good for relieving problems such as bloating, cellulite and pre-menstrual syndrome (PMS). It is also very relaxing.

Sacral Chakra Meditation

Meditating on – and in – water has a powerful and positive effect on the sacral chakra. The heat and support of the water relaxes your body, and your mind becomes still to focus on the meditation.

This is an unusual meditation because it takes place in water and incorporates the sensations of water into the meditation. It is important that the water is warm, and stays warm, as the meditation may last for 20 minutes. One way of ensuring this is to add a spoonful of warming spices, such as ginger, sage and cayenne pepper, to the water. If you find these too heating, try Dead Sea salts or a few drops of a relaxing essential oil, such as rose, lavender or sandalwood. You can also use Epsom salts, which are full of magnesium and which will help your joints and muscles to relax.

You can do the water meditation in a bath at home, but it's also wonderful to do in a flotation tank. The first time I tried flotation, I was expecting it to be claustrophobic but, after the first 15 minutes, I found myself totally at ease in my watery environment. I turned out the lights and floated contentedly for the rest of my allotted hour. Unless you happen to be an astronaut, floating in water is the only time that your body is free of the forces of gravity, and it is an extraordinary feeling. The combination of weightlessness and the absence of external stimuli enables the body to relax and the mind to become still. External stimuli – gravity, temperature, touch, sight, sound – account for 90 per cent of normal neuro-muscular activity. When they are absent, even for an hour, the brain and nervous system can achieve a state that is not only relaxing, but rebalancing. Activity in the left, logical side of the brain reduces, while activity in the right, creative side increases.

WATER MEDITATION

Spend some time preparing your bathroom before you do this meditation. Run a warm bath, light some candles and make sure that you have some warm towels and a bath robe for when you come out of the bath. If you can, find a tape or CD recording of water — the sound of the sea or a fountain, or the music of whales is ideal. Play this softly in the background to help you meditate.

Get into the bath and submerge yourself in the water. Let go of any tension in your muscles and find a position in which your body can relax completely.

Breathe in deeply through your nose, bring the air down into your belly, hold it for a few moments and then exhale slowly through your mouth. Repeat this three times and then let yourself breathe normally. Close your eyes and bring your attention to your breath. Don't count your breath — just observe how your breath enters and leaves your body.

Now bring your consciousness to focus on the water around you. Feel the touch of it on your body, how it moves and responds to your breathing, its warmth, and how it supports your body. Observe how the water brings calmness and relaxation. Extend your consciousness to visualize the great bodies of water that cover most of the planet — the lakes, the seas and the oceans. Sense the rhythm of the waves and their gentle lapping on the shore. Visualize the moon's pull on the water, drawing the tides up and down. Picture yourself floating on a calm sea under a bright moon. Do this for at least five minutes, focusing on the sensation of the water holding and supporting you, and the pale moonlight shining down on you. Feel the moon pulling the tides of your body toward her and feel a sense of being at one with the waters of the world.

Gradually bring your awareness back to the water around you and your breath. Focus on your breathing for a few minutes, then slowly open your eyes and take in your surroundings. Feel the sense of tranquillity and relaxation that comes from water meditation. When you are ready, get out of the bath, pat yourself dry, dress in a warm robe and go to bed or rest for at least half an hour.

The Solar Plexus Chakra

Manipura

The solar plexus chakra is extremely complex. It is the chakra of the mind, ruling rational thought, discernment and individuality. Yet it is also a very physical chakra, governing your digestive system, liver and spleen, as well as your back. It is the chakra from which your moral judgments emerge, and from which you draw the moral courage to stand up for what you believe in.

An overly dominant solar plexus chakra leads to bullying, egotistical and aggressive behaviour. A weak solar plexus chakra results in fear, guilt and lack of confidence. When your solar plexus chakra is in balance, you are discerning, disciplined and assertive, and you face life's challenges with courage and integrity.

About the Solar Plexus Chakra

This chakra is in your navel area and relates to your abdominal organs, particularly your digestive system. Ailments resulting from an unbalanced solar plexus chakra include ulcers, irritable bowel syndrome, liver and digestive problems. Fasting (see page 62) is a good way to balance this chakra.

The Sanskrit name for the solar plexus chakra, Manipura, means "jewel in the city", and the jewel it refers to is the mind. When your solar plexus chakra is in balance, your mind is also in balance. You are in control of yourself and the challenges and decisions that you face in life. You see yourself as a separate individual – not just part of a group or a partnership – and you express that individuality with integrity, and treat everyone you meet as equals.

In contrast, angry, controlling behaviour and ruthless ambition, are the signs of a dominant solar plexus chakra. This dominance can turn people into workaholics with power and conflict at the centre of their lives. They may be abrasive and feel the need to battle over very minor issues. At worst people may be violent.

A weak solar plexus chakra creates feelings of insecurity and guilt and makes people unable to stand up for themselves. Those with underdeveloped solar plexus chakras are easily manipulated and are governed by perceived pecking orders and what other people might think of them. They tend not to like their own company and are in need of constant reassurance.

As its name suggests, the solar plexus chakra is governed by the sun and, when it is in balance, it is reflected in an almost tangible radiance. As well as being warm in nature, people with balanced solar plexus chakras also have a healthy intuition – they can generally rely on their hunches or "gut instincts" – and they can express themselves well.

Because the solar plexus chakra is the the centre of the intellect and decision-making, it is important for the health and development of this chakra that you make your own choices, rather than have them made for you. The development of the solar plexus chakra is hindered if you have a feeling of powerlessness in life. This feeling can be common in adults who, as children, grew up feeling that they had no say in making decisions. Feelings of disempowerment can happen at any age, however, not just during childhood.

The developmental age associated with the solar plexus chakra is eight to 12. Marking the end of this time period with a special rite of passage that ushers in puberty is important for the health and balance of the solar plexus chakra.

Yoga to Stimulate the Solar Plexus Chakra

The following yoga postures stimulate your solar plexus chakra by engaging your abdominal muscles. The postures also employ a powerful muscular lock called uddiyana bandha.

The Boat

The Boat, or Navasana, owes its name to the V-shape of a simple boat. It strengthens both your abdominal and your back muscles, and improves balance and focus.

Uddiyana Bandha

This is the strongest of the three yogic bandhas or locks (see page 28). Uddiyana means "upward flying" and to engage this bandha, you exhale completely and then lift your lower abdominal muscles simultaneously upward and inward. At the same time you should make sure that your rib cage is pulled down.

1 Sit on the floor with your spine long and straight, your legs straight in front of you and your toes pointed. Check that there is no tension in your neck or shoulders.

2 Breathe in and, as you breathe out, engage the mula and uddiyana bandhas. Keeping your legs together (from the tops of your thighs down to your feet), lift them straight up so that your body forms a V-shape. You can use your hands to help support your legs.

3 Keep your balance by firmly engaging the uddiyana bandha, then position your arms so that they are parallel to the floor. Gaze straight ahead – if your spine is as straight as it should be, you will be looking at your toes. Hold this position for five long, slow breaths. Focus on uddiyana bandha to help maintain your balance.

First Open Balance

This balance follows on naturally from The Boat. Again, the way to keep your balance is a combination of visual focus and a strong engagement of the bandhas.

1 Sit with your legs out in front of you and then draw your knees toward you. Take hold of your toes in your fingers, bend your knees in to your chest and slowly extend your legs — your aim, over time, is to straighten them. Engage the uddiyana bandha. When you have extended your legs as far as you can, take five long, deep breaths in this position.

2 When you feel confident holding your balance in this position — or even before you feel confident! — try this next stage. From the extended leg position, exhale and roll back, taking your legs over your head. Breathe in and, as you breathe out again, roll back up in one continuous movement. This is the difficult bit. You may find that you get only part of the way up and get stuck. However, the more you do this rolling posture, the stronger your uddiyana bandha becomes and the more your balance and confidence will improve.

Second Open Balance

In this balance your legs are open instead of parallel. If you feel daring, you can also extend this balance into a rolling posture, although make sure that you can do the First Open Balance competently first.

Sit with your legs out in front of you and then draw your knees toward you. Take hold of your toes in your fingers, bend your knees in to your chest and slowly extend your legs out to the sides. Again, your eventual aim is to extend them fully but, at first, just go as far as is comfortable. The most important part of this exercise is keeping your balance. Engage the uddiyana bandha and focus ahead of you and slightly upward by about 45 degrees.

Downward-facing Dog

This pose, known in Sanskrit as Adho Mukha Svanasana, develops your strength and is good for your lower back. Although you may tend to concentrate on other aspects of the pose, it is essential that you engage the uddiyana bandha to give the posture strength and a firm foundation. Downward-facing Dog doesn't have the same beneficial effects if your abdominal muscles are not engaged.

1 Begin on your hands and knees, preferably in front of a mirror. Check that your arms are straight and your hands are beneath your shoulders. Your knees should be hip-width apart and, most importantly, your back should be flat rather than concave or convex. Breathe in and, as you breathe out, engage the uddiyana bandha and keep it engaged for the rest of the posture.

2 Tuck your toes under and on your next out-breath lift your hips up so that your body forms an inverted V-shape. Keep your neck in line with your spine and press your heels down into the floor. Take five long, deep breaths in this position, each time trying to straighten your legs further and push your upper body as far as it will go through your arms. Many people, particularly women whose arm strength may be less developed than men's, find this posture quite hard on the wrists. If your wrists ache or feel as though they are burning, spend a little time rotating them in each direction when you come out of the pose.

First Twist

This twisting posture effectively massages the abdominal area and the internal organs, such as the stomach, kidneys and spleen.

1 Sit with your legs out in front of you and your back long and straight. Bend your left knee so that it rests on the floor with the left foot tucked up by your right thigh. Cross your right leg over the top of your left, with your right foot on the floor.

2 Breathe in and, as you breathe out, engage the uddiyana bandha, lengthen your spine and rotate around your spine so that you are facing over your right hip. Without sacrificing the straightness of your spine, keep rotating to try to look behind you. You can increase the stretch by pressing your left arm against your raised right thigh. When you have reached your fullest stretch, make sure that there is no tension in your back or shoulders and take five long, slow breaths in this position.

Second Twist

This twist is extremely relaxing and a good way to end any yoga session.

Lie on your back for this twist. Bend your knees and rest your feet on the floor. Keeping your knees and ankles together, let your knees drop over to the left toward the floor. Turn your head to the right and take at least five long, slow breaths or just relax into the posture for as long as possible. Repeat on the other side of your body.

Chi Gong to Stimulate the Solar Plexus Chakra

The power behind these two exercises comes from the solar plexus chakra, so engage your abdominal muscles as you begin.

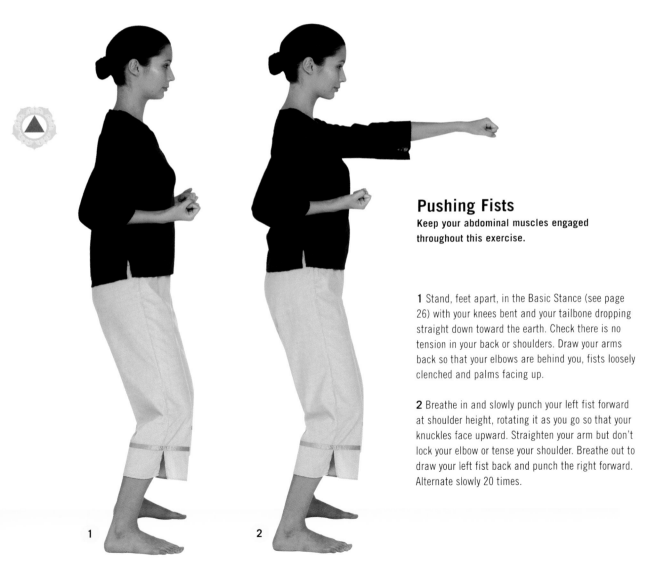

Pushing Fists

Keep your abdominal muscles engaged throughout this exercise.

1 Stand, feet apart, in the Basic Stance (see page 26) with your knees bent and your tailbone dropping straight down toward the earth. Check there is no tension in your back or shoulders. Draw your arms back so that your elbows are behind you, fists loosely clenched and palms facing up.

2 Breathe in and slowly punch your left fist forward at shoulder height, rotating it as you go so that your knuckles face upward. Straighten your arm but don't lock your elbow or tense your shoulder. Breathe out to draw your left fist back and punch the right forward. Alternate slowly 20 times.

1

2

Pushing Palms

Before you try the arm movements of Pushing Palms, practise simply shifting your weight from one foot to the other, as described in steps 1 to 3.

1 Stand with your left foot about 46 cm (18 in) in front of the right. Turn your right foot out and keep your left foot facing directly forward. Bend your knees and distribute your weight evenly over both feet. This is Bow Stance. Cross your hands in front of you.

2 Breathe in and shift your weight back on to your right foot, bending your right knee more deeply and straightening your left knee. As you do so raise the toes of your left foot (but leave the heel on the ground) and bend your elbows, drawing your forearms up so that your hands are relaxed and level with your shoulders.

3 Breathe out, transfer your weight forward on to your left foot and lift your right heel. Push your hands forward, palms facing in front, as if you are pushing something away from you.

4 Breathe in and draw your arms back so that you are in the same position as step 2. Repeat steps 3 and 4 slowly up to 20 times and then repeat with your right foot in front.

Strengthening the Abdominal Muscles

The abdominal muscles are governed by the solar plexus chakra, and the following exercises aim to strengthen these muscles. Strong abdominal muscles contribute to good posture. They also help to prevent back and neck injury, and they protect your internal organs. Avoid pushing yourself too hard – stop if you feel any strain in your back or if your muscles start to quiver.

Abdominal Toners
Practise these movements regularly. Start slowly and gently.

1 Lie on your back with your knees raised and your feet flat on the floor. Your entire spine should be flat on the floor, with your neck long and in line with your spine – you may need to tilt your chin down slightly to achieve this. Check there is no tension in your shoulders. Rest your arms by your sides.

2 Take a deep breath and, as you breathe out, draw your navel to your spine, engaging the yogic lock known as uddiyana bandha (see page 54). Become aware of the small of your back on the floor. Squeeze the muscles at the base of your buttocks (not your thighs) and very slowly, start to curl up off the floor, bringing your buttocks and lower back up in a scooped-out shape. Check that no tension has crept into your shoulders. Peel up as far as you can, keeping the movement slow and focused. Return to the floor in the same way as you came up and repeat the movement 10 times.

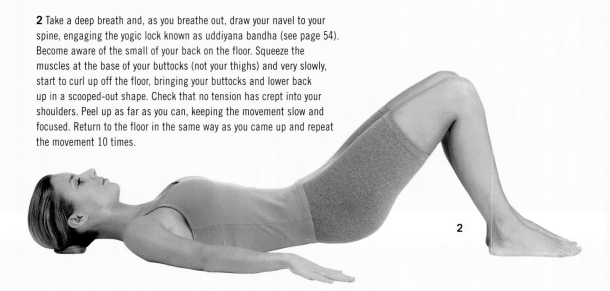

3 Return to the starting position and place your hands on your thighs. Breathe in and, as you breathe out, engage your abdominal muscles and slowly start to walk your fingers up your thighs toward your knees. As you do so your head and shoulders will start to curl up off the floor. Don't expect to come up very high. It is more important to use your abdominal muscles correctly than it is to come up off the floor. When your fingers have reached as far as they can, place your hands flat on your thighs, breathe in, and slide your hands down your thighs and uncurl back down to the floor. Repeat this movement 10 times.

4 Return to the starting position and place your left hand under your head and your right arm by your side on the floor. Breathe in and, as you breathe out, engage your abdominal muscles and slowly reach your right hand down the floor toward your feet. This will make your head and left shoulder curl up off the floor. Go only as far as you can, maintaining a concave navel. Curl back down and repeat, this time on the other side. Build up to 10 repetitions each side.

Balancing the Solar Plexus Chakra

The solar plexus chakra is strongly associated with food and digestion. One of the best ways to work on this chakra is to cleanse the digestive system and allow it to rest by fasting. This is the oldest form of healing known to man.

As with all the chakras, the physical aspects of the solar plexus chakra are intimately related to its mental and emotional aspects. Just as the stomach and intestines are busy digesting food most of the time, so the mind is busy digesting stimuli from the outside world. The benefit of fasting is that your mind, as well as your digestive system, is able to rest. A fast is a valuable opportunity to bring your focus inward; it is good for contemplation and is practised in most meditating communities. Just as a bad diet builds up toxins and waste throughout your body, negative emotions can get stored up, too. Fasting helps you to let go.

There are two main ways to fast. You can drink water and nothing else, in which case you should fast for just one day. Spend this day drinking plenty of water to flush out the toxins – a minimum of 2 litres (3.5 pints) – and rest as much as you can. The alternative – a juice fast – is my preferred method. Vitamins and minerals in juices have a more immediate cleansing impact than water alone. You will need to buy a

THREE-DAY JUICE FAST

For two or three days before fasting, eat only raw food, drink plenty of water or herbal tea and one vegetable and one fruit juice a day. Avoid caffeine, alcohol and cigarettes. On fasting days: rise early; exercise; drink four large glasses of organic juice, plus water and herbal tea; scrub your skin and use alternating showers (see pages 46–7); meditate; and go to bed early.

Morning juices: Choose any or all of these in combination: carrot, beetroot, broccoli and spinach.

Lunchtime juices: Choose any fruits you like. Pawpaw, pineapple, mango and melon mixed with berries and apple are delicious.

Afternoon juice: Drink a combination of carrot and apple juice.

Evening juice: Drink a calming lettuce-based juice to aid sleep. Add an apple, a couple of tomatoes or beetroot, and a carrot or red pepper for variety.

SOLAR THERAPY

The sun's energy is vital to the solar plexus chakra and walking in the sunshine is very balancing for this chakra. If you can't be in the sun because it's midwinter and the sky is grey, sit in front of a real fire (fire is this chakra's element). Alternatively, spend time in a room that is painted bright yellow (this is the colour of the solar plexus chakra). You can also fill vases with yellow lilies or tulips, or spend an evening in a room lit with yellow candles.

The following crystals are useful for doing work on the solar plexus chakra: sunstone, yellow citrine, calcite, iron pyrites (fool's gold) or topaz. At a time when you are sure there won't be any distractions, lie down on the floor in a peaceful space. Place your chosen crystal on your solar plexus chakra – on your navel – and allow your body to completely relax. Visualize the sun's warm, golden radiance transmitting itself through the crystal and cleansing you of any negative thoughts or feelings. Let the sun fill you with strength and warmth, and then allow these feelings to flow out to all living beings. While you are in this warm and giving state, ask the warmth of the sun to help you overcome any problem you might have, whether it's to do with your insecurities, problems in your personal life or difficulties at work. If you can do this visualization outdoors lying beneath the actual sun, so much the better.

juicer to make your own fresh juices, but this is a worthwhile investment as one or two fresh juices a day will have a beneficial effect on your general health. The juice fast opposite is for three days but you can also do it for a longer or shorter period of time. For optimum results you should do a juice fast two to four times a year.

Ideally, you should be on your own during a fast, or with others who are also fasting. Take time out and tune in to your body. If you want to walk in the fresh air, then go. If you feel tired, lie down and sleep. The following essential oils help to balance the solar plexus chakra and are good to use during a fast: rosemary, juniper, geranium, peppermint, bergamot and cinnamon.

Fasting may cause side-effects, such as headaches, a coated tongue and skin eruptions. These are simply signs that the body is eliminating toxins. There are also pleasant side-effects, such as a bloom in the skin, silky soft hair and bright, clear eyes. Check with a doctor before fasting, and avoid fasting if you are pregnant or breast-feeding, or if you have a serious illness.

Agni – the Digestive Fire
According to Ayurveda (traditional Indian medicine), the body's ability to digest and metabolize food is governed by agni, the digestive force or fire found in the solar plexus chakra. For healthy agni you should eat your main meal at lunch, eat lightly at breakfast and supper, and avoid snacking. Always eat slowly, and don't overeat – you should be only three-quarters full after a meal. Never eat while working or watching television. After eating, take a short five- or ten-minute walk to aid digestion.

Solar Plexus Chakra Meditation

Fiercely held emotions are stored in the solar plexus chakra – think of the term "gut reaction". An unbalanced solar plexus chakra will result in emotions that are thoughtless, violent or desperate. This meditation helps you to let go of strong, negative emotions and brings the solar plexus chakra into balance.

This meditation uses the colours of each individual chakra and it restores balance to all of the chakras. Many people find this one of the most delightful and relaxing meditations to practise.

As you meditate upon each of the chakras, it is important that you visualize the colours as bright and clear and lit with their own inner light – rather than muddy or dark. Try to bring your entire focus to each of the colours and see it flooding through you as it whirls out from each of the spinning chakras.

This colour meditation moves gradually up the column of chakras, starting at the root and ending at the crown, and so follows the course of kundalini (see pages 10–11). You may experience kundalini in a physical way, as a release or a flow of energy. Sometimes, if kundalini is ignited, you might have a very strong reaction. If you feel overwhelmed, bring your focus back to your breathing and try meditating on each chakra individually rather than one after the other.

The solar plexus chakra governs the ability to learn and when it is blocked you are likely to be unfocused. As well as releasing strongly held negative emotions, this meditation can also restore mental focus, increase your ability to concentrate, and enhance learning.

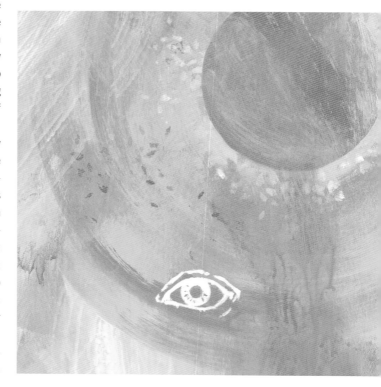

COLOUR MEDITATION

Sit in a comfortable position with your back straight and take a few moments to settle yourself. Bring your focus to your breath and observe the air entering your body, bringing its life-giving oxygen to every cell, and then leaving, taking with it all distractions and irrelevant thoughts. Now bring your focus to the chakras, lying in a line from the root to the crown and pulsing with your vital energy. Visualize each one in turn as a spinning circle of colour. Spend several minutes on each chakra before moving on to the next.

Start by imagining the red circle of the root chakra. Visualize its grounding energy. Make the circle spin faster and feel safe and secure in the power that roots you to the earth.

Now see the bright orange of the sacral chakra. As it spins brighter and faster, feel how it strengthens the love you have for not your ego, but for your true inner self.

Visualize the solar plexus chakra as a spinning circle of the brightest yellow. Let the circle spin away jealousy, anger, despair, hatred or any other negative emotions that you are holding on to. Now see it fuelled by positive feelings of tranquillity and happiness that make it spin brighter and faster.

See the rose pink colour of the heart chakra. Send out a feeling of unconditional love that asks nothing in return.

Imagine the clear blue of the throat chakra. Visualize it drawing in and sending out true, harmonious communication, linking you to all living creatures.

Now move to the brow chakra with its spinning circle of deep, vibrant indigo. Picture it spinning to the music of your still, focused mind and body.

Finally, take your focus to the crown chakra with its pure violet light spinning in a circle of tranquillity, peace and oneness with the greater spirit.

Mentally stand back and watch all of these seven chakra wheels spinning together with light and unity. Watch them as they restore balance to your body and mind, lighten your heart and open your spirit.

The Heart Chakra

Anahata

The heart chakra is at the centre of the column of seven chakras. Below it, the root, sacral and solar plexus chakras represent the personal and the physical. Above it, the throat, brow and crown chakras represent the spiritual and universal. The heart chakra provides the vital link for the whole.

Essentially, your heart chakra is associated with love and compassion – not just the love you feel for a partner or a child, but a love of God and all creation. When your heart chakra is out of balance, you may lack confidence and be unable to let go of your fears. When your heart chakra is balanced, you feel energized and have the strength to fulfil your hopes and dreams, and to give and receive unconditional love.

About the Heart Chakra

The heart chakra is situated in the centre of your body and its dominion extends to your lungs, your ribcage, your arms, your hands and your upper back. Being the central chakra it acts as the fundamental link between the physical and the transcendental, the body and the spirit.

Visually, the heart chakra's lotus flower has 12 blue or green petals. The colours associated with this chakra are green, rose pink and the deeper, blue-pink of rose amethyst. This chakra is also symbolized by a six-pointed star, although one that is indistinct, as if seen through smoke.

The element of the heart chakra is air, but its sense is touch – another balancing of the ethereal with the physical. The hands are closely associated with the heart chakra, and a kind touch is an outward sign of the love, compassion and forgiveness that typify this chakra when it is in an open and balanced state. Massage is a perfect example of how love can be given through the hands from an open heart chakra.

The heart chakra is also a seat of creativity. A blocked heart chakra results in creative blocks, while an open one leaves you open to inspiration.

However, the heart chakra can be too open. You can pour out so much heart energy in your desire to help others that you can have none left for yourself. You end up stressed and drained.

The key, as ever, is balance. The heart, in common with all the chakras, needs to have its own flexibility, the ability to open and close as necessary. This is particularly important in the heart as it is the chakra of change, giving us the confidence to fulfil our hopes, make a break with the past, and embrace the future.

Physically, the heart chakra is connected to the thymus gland, which is part of the lymphatic system, which in turn is central to the immune system. A blocked or poorly functioning heart chakra can lead to a weakened immune system, stress-related disorders and problems involving the lungs and respiratory system.

The yoga and meditation exercises recommended for rebalancing the heart chakra follow, but there are other methods, too, that will help in the process. Massage is beneficial, especially if you use one of the essential oils associated with the heart chakra, such as rose, jasmine and neroli. Particular crystals are also associated with the heart chakra. They include rose quartz, rose and green tourmaline, emerald, jade, and pink carnelian.

Yoga to Stimulate the Heart Chakra

These yoga poses are particularly suited to balancing the heart chakra. They open and expand your chest, deepen your breathing, ease stress and liberate your emotions.

Crescent Moon Pose

Known as Ardha Chandrasana in Sanskrit, Crescent Moon Pose is a strong pose for opening your chest and enhancing its flexibility and resilience. As well as energizing your body, it helps it to recover from emotional demands.

1 Start on all fours with your hands directly beneath your shoulders, your knees in line with your hips, and your back flat. Breathe in and, as you breathe out, draw your abdominal muscles in and stretch one leg out behind you. Bring the other to join it so that you are in a press-up position. Keep your back flat and your abdominal muscles engaged.

2 Breathe in and bring your left leg forward so that the shin is vertical and the knee is as close to your chest as possible. Tuck your tailbone under and keep your abdominal muscles engaged. Be careful not to strain your lower back. Drop your right knee to the floor. Relax your right foot so that your toes are flat on the floor, and relax your shoulders and neck.

USING PRANA

When performing the Crescent Moon Pose, it is important to remember that as well as opening your heart centre, you are also encouraging the flow of prana. Kundalini energy flows along a pathway (nadi) very close to your spinal cord and so you are trying to keep the channel free from obstruction. To do this you need to keep your spine extended – even though this is a back bend, your spine should be long and strong. Do not let your lower back collapse or let tension creep into your shoulders. Instead, reach out of your lower back and let your raised arms take their strength from your middle back, rather than by lifting your shoulders. If you focus on opening the front of your body – as if you were trying to push your heart chakra toward the ceiling – this will help keep your back in the correct position.

3 Breathe out and use your abdominal muscles to raise your body to a tall and lifted vertical position. Make sure that there is no tension in your shoulders or jaw and that you are not arching your lower back. Rest your right hand on your bent knee. Take a long breath in and out and feel the stretch.

Breathe in and raise your arms above your head, keeping your upper back and your chest open – the secret is to keep your abdominal muscles strong and to move your arms from the centre of your back, not your shoulders.

4 Look up to the ceiling and bring your palms together. Hold the pose for a minute or two, breathing slowly. When you are ready, breathe in and as you breathe out, drop your hands to the floor, take your leg back behind you, as in step 1, and repeat on the other side of your body.

The Fish

This posture, known in Sanskrit as Matsyasana, opens up the throat chakra as well as the heart chakra. It strengthens your spine and your breathing, but you should avoid it if you have neck problems.

1 Lie on your back with a long, straight spine and your legs stretched out in front of you, feet pointed. Place your hands, palms down, underneath you.

2 Breathe in and, as you breathe out, draw your abdominal muscles to your navel. Breathe in and bend your elbows to raise your chest to the ceiling and open your ribs. Drop your head behind you. Keep your legs strong and straight.

3 Let the crown of your head touch the floor behind you, but don't put any weight on it. Support your head by pulling up through your abdomen and ribs. Hold this position for a minute or two then relax back down onto the floor.

Side Forward Bend

This posture opens up the front of your chest and is also a good stretch for your back and legs. As in the Forward Bends on pages 24–5, you should bend by folding or hinging from your hips rather than by rounding your back. Keep your back straight throughout the posture, even if it means that you will not be able to reach so far.

1 Stand with your feet about 1 metre (3 feet) apart, your toes facing forward and your neck and shoulders relaxed. Breathe in and, as you breathe out, engage the mula and uddiyana bandhas (see pages 28 and 54). Take your hands behind your back and place them, palms together, in prayer position, as high up your back as they will go.

2 Breathe in and turn your right foot out to a 90-degree angle. Slightly turn in your left foot and turn your body so that your hips are square and you are facing your right leg. If you want to increase the stretch at this point, you can arch your lower back slightly so you look up toward the ceiling. As you breathe out bend from your hips over your right leg. Keep your back straight. Don't overextend your knee, but try to keep your legs straight. Take the stretch as long and low as you can. Take five long, slow breaths. Return to standing and repeat on the other side of your body.

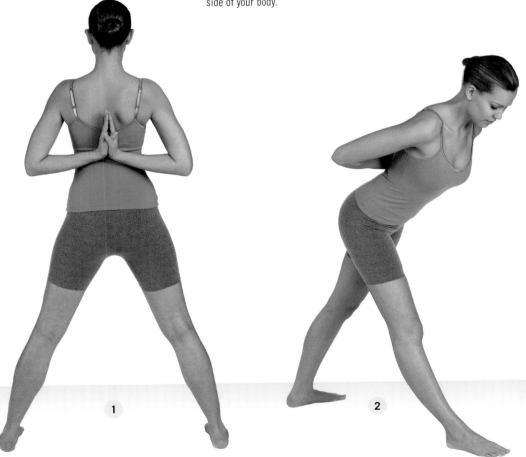

Chi Gong to Stimulate the Heart Chakra

These two exercises work to open up the heart chakra and stimulate the lungs and the circulation. They also have an uplifting effect emotionally and are particularly beneficial for anyone suffering from anxiety or depression.

Separating the Clouds

Make your arm movements slow and fluid and synchronize the movements with your breath.

1 Begin in the Basic Stance (see page 26) with your knees bent and your shoulders relaxed. Breathe in and, as you breathe out, deepen the bend in your knees without lifting your heels off the floor. Bring your hands in front of you so that they cross at the wrists level with your navel.

2 Breathe in and slowly straighten your knees, raising your crossed arms up in front of you until they are above your head.

3 Breathe out, uncross your arms and lower them until they are straight out to the sides, bending your knees as you do so. Draw your arms to the front, and cross them at the wrists again. Repeat the whole movement slowly up to 20 times.

Flying Dove

Imagine that your arms are encircling a large beach ball in this exercise.

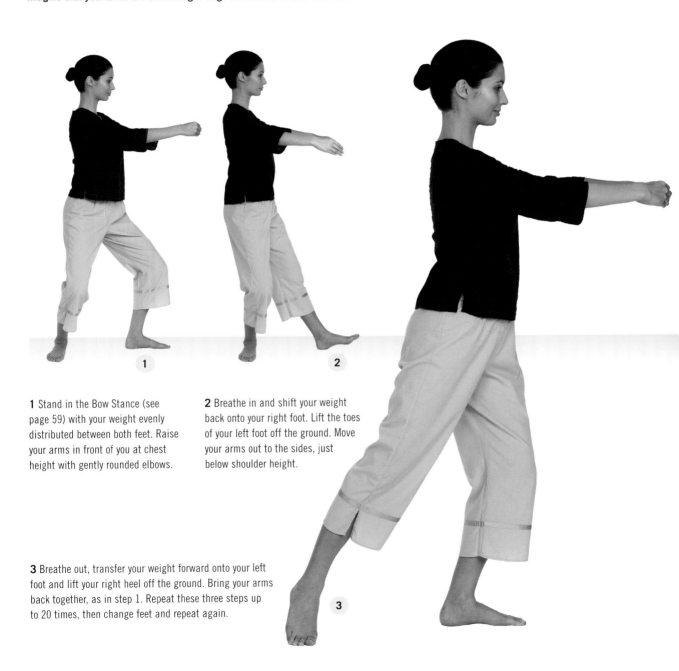

1 Stand in the Bow Stance (see page 59) with your weight evenly distributed between both feet. Raise your arms in front of you at chest height with gently rounded elbows.

2 Breathe in and shift your weight back onto your right foot. Lift the toes of your left foot off the ground. Move your arms out to the sides, just below shoulder height.

3 Breathe out, transfer your weight forward onto your left foot and lift your right heel off the ground. Bring your arms back together, as in step 1. Repeat these three steps up to 20 times, then change feet and repeat again.

Balancing the Heart Chakra

The heart chakra governs love, compassion and creativity. Two wonderful ways to bring this chakra into balance are to use your hands to deliver loving, caring touch in the form of massage and to find a form of creative expression for yourself. Breathing exercises, such as alternate nostril breathing, can also have a powerfully therapuetic effect on the heart chakra.

The Hand Chakras

The hands have an important role in balancing the heart chakra because they contain secondary chakras that are directly connected to the heart chakra. Love, compassion and affection express themselves through both the heart and the hands, and the hand chakras allow the heart chakra's energy to flow. The hand chakras are also closely linked to another important aspect of the heart chakra: creativity. We often express ourselves creatively through our hands; for example, by playing an instrument, cooking or drawing a picture.

The hand chakras are used to great therapeutic effect in massage and this is something anyone can do. You don't have to be trained in massage therapy – you just need to tune in to the healing power of your hands. The full-body aromatherapy massage on the opposite page is an excellent place to start. Because massage is such a powerful therapy, your hands may soak up the negativity that your partner loses during the massage – for this reason it is a good idea to wash your hands in cold water for a minute or two when you have finished giving a massage.

Crystal Meditation

To bring your hand chakras into greater touch with your heart chakra, try meditating using some of the heart's crystals, such as rose quartz (see page 68 for other examples). Take one crystal in each hand. Sit quietly with your eyes closed and feel the crystals resting in the centre of your palms where the hand chakras are situated. Sense the crystals' energy opening up the hand chakras and flowing up through your arms and into your heart chakra. Feel the energy from your heart chakra flowing back down through your arms and out through the hand chakras into the world. Sit in this way for ten minutes allowing the connection to build between your hand and your heart chakras.

Express Yourself Creatively

The heart chakra is a store of creativity, and the more you express yourself creatively, the more open your heart chakra becomes. Creativity can be anything you want it to be – you don't have to have a carefully honed product to show for your efforts and you don't have to make something beautiful or artistic. You don't even

AROMATHERAPY MASSAGE

Giving or receiving a massage is a particularly good way of opening your heart chakra. Massage combines two important heart elements: physical touch, involving the all-important hand chakras, and the heart's gift of sharing. Unlike the root chakra, which benefits from strenuous massage, the heart chakra benefits from a massage that is slow and gentle. A massage that uses essential oils is especially effective, as these relax and open up the heart centre even more. Sweet, sensual oils such as rose, sandalwood, bergamot and jasmine suit the heart chakra best. The following techniques are easy to do and you can share the experience with a friend, taking turns to give and receive the massage.

You need a warm, comfortable room for massage. Create subtle lighting using candles, or dim the lights. Make sure there won't be any interruptions: turn off telephones and hang a "do not disturb" sign on the door. If you don't have a massage table or a very firm bed, lay out lots of towels on the floor and have some warm towels ready to cover those parts of your partner's body you're not working on.

To make the massage oil, add 25 drops of your chosen essential oil to 50 ml (2 fl oz) of a carrier oil, such as almond or olive. Warm the oil in your palms before you apply it. After the massage, cover your partner with warm towels and leave them to relax for at least ten minutes.

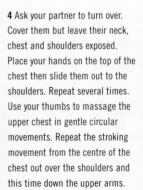

1 Ask your partner to lie face down. Cover their body with towels, except for their right leg. Slide your oiled hands up the centre of the right leg then all the way down the outside. Repeat several times.

2 Using your thumbs, massage around the right ankle bone and then up the leg, pressing with your thumbs as you go. At the top, stroke your way down the outer leg to the ankle. Repeat steps 1 and 2 on the left leg.

3 Uncover your partner's back and stroke from the base of the spine up to the neck, then over the shoulders and down again. Gently press your thumbs on the muscles on either side of the spine and knead the neck muscles. Slide your palms down from the neck to the base of the spine, over the tops of the buttocks and back up the sides. Repeat several times, gradually reducing the pressure each time. Finish with a feather-light stroke.

4 Ask your partner to turn over. Cover them but leave their neck, chest and shoulders exposed. Place your hands on the top of the chest then slide them out to the shoulders. Repeat several times. Use your thumbs to massage the upper chest in gentle circular movements. Repeat the stroking movement from the centre of the chest out over the shoulders and this time down the upper arms.

5 Lift your partner's arm and place their hand on your leg as you kneel beside them. Stroke oil all the way up the arm. Circle your thumbs on the arm and on the palm of the hand. Gently pull each finger. Repeat on the other arm.

6 Uncover the right leg and gently stroke the whole foot. Circle your thumbs on the sole. Pull out and gently stretch each toe. Firmly knead the calf and thigh muscles. Repeat on the other leg.

have to produce anything at all. The joy is in the act rather than in the outcome. Here are some ideas:

- Write a poem.
- Make a cake.
- Find a piece of music that speaks to you and dance to it.
- Paint or sketch a portrait of your child, pet, partner, parent or friend.
- Play a musical instrument.
- Make up a story or play word association inside your head.
- Build or make something out of wood or clay.
- Take a camera with you when you go out. Look in detail at your surroundings and photograph the things that interest you or catch your eye.
- Pick up a pen or some coloured pencils and start doodling.
- Plant some flowers in your garden.

To enjoy creative acts try to let go of your inhibitions and just enjoy doing something for the sake of it.

Alternate Nostril Breathing

This is an invigorating and energizing yoga breathing exercise. It draws a great deal of oxygen into your system and clears your mind. The hand position you use is known as Vishnu mudra. To do Vishnu mudra, fold the index and middle fingers of your right hand into your palm.

It is important to keep your spine straight throughout this exercise – you can either sit cross-legged on the floor if your back is strong enough, or you can simply sit in a chair with your feet flat on the floor.

1 Lift your right hand so that it is level with your face. Make the Vishnu mudra position. Close your eyes and breathe in. Using your thumb, close your right nostril and exhale slowly through your left nostril. Inhale again through your left nostril.

2 Now release your right nostril and close your left nostril with the fourth and fifth fingers of your right hand. Exhale and then inhale through your right nostril. Repeat steps 1 and 2 up to ten times.

THE POSITIVE POWER OF LAUGHTER

Laughter opens up the heart and, in turn, an open heart is more able to laugh – this is a particularly virtuous circle! Laughter has also been shown to have beneficial effects on a number of serious diseases, including high blood pressure, heart disease and even cancer. Some books have the power to make you laugh out loud (Stella Gibbons' *Cold Comfort Farm* and Jerome K. Jerome's *Three Men in a Boat* work for me). Or you can watch funny films or plays, or go to see a stand-up comedian where you get to share your laughter with others. Laughter makes you feel good and has been shown to reduce stress. As adults we often forget how to play and enjoy simple fun and laughter. If you have children, try to take time out from the role of supervising – get down to your child's level and play a game. This could be a rough-and-tumble game, a make-believe game or a messy, outdoors game. You can even play dressing-up. If you don't have children, play with the children of friends or family members, or make friends with a puppy or a kitten!

Samanu

Samanu is a technique that combines alternate nostril breathing with visualization. Try it at the end of your yoga practice, or simply by itself.

1 Sit in a comfortable, upright position with a long, straight spine. Take three long, slow breaths to settle your mind.

2 Take your focus to the heart chakra. Using your fingers in the same way as for alternate nostril breathing, breathe in through your left nostril. Feel the breath reach your heart. Close both nostrils, retain your breath and visualize it filling your heart. Exhale through your right nostril.

3 Breathe in through your right nostril. This time visualize your breath reaching the solar plexus chakra. Close both nostrils, retain your breath and visualize it filling your navel area. Exhale through your left nostril. Repeat three times. Try to extend the length of the breath retention.

RELAXING BREATH

This exercise slows your heart rate and pulse. Try it at the end of a yoga session or at any time when you feel stressed and need to relax. If counting slowly to five is difficult at first, begin with a count of three. As you become more accomplished, make the central section of the exercise – the holding of your breath – ten counts.

Lie on your back on the floor in Corpse Pose (see page 134). Let your legs relax completely and check that your neck and spine are in a straight line. Place your hands on either side of your abdomen so that your fingertips just touch. Take a long, slow breath through your nose counting slowly to five. Your lungs and abdomen will expand, making your fingertips part. Hold your breath for a further count of five. Slowly exhale through your mouth to a count of ten, trying to empty your body of air completely. Repeat this complete breath up to ten times.

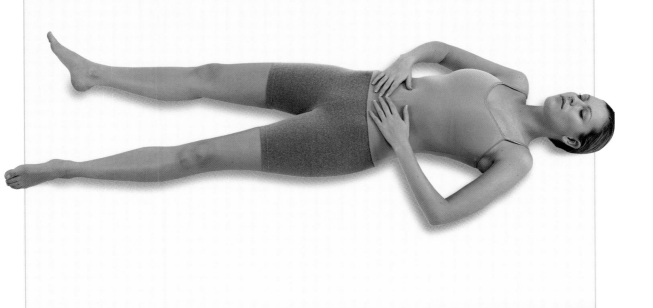

Heart Chakra Meditation

In the Buddhist tradition compassion encompasses the desire to love all beings equally. By focusing on your heart chakra in meditation, you can open your heart and encourage the development of compassion.

The heart chakra is strongly linked with positive emotions, such as love and compassion. This meditation is designed to develop these feelings and it is based on one I learned at the Tibetan Buddhist monastery of Kopan in the foothills of the Nepalese Himalaya. Like many of the guided Buddhist meditations, it is very demanding on an emotional and spiritual level. It is therefore best to build up to it slowly, meditating on each section for at least five or six sessions before extending it to embrace the next step. It is also a good idea to make a recording of each section in advance. Doing this enables you to focus on the meditation as you listen to the words, rather than struggling to remember what you should be doing in each step. At whichever point you finish your meditation, bring your mind back to watching your breath for a few minutes before you slowly open your eyes.

You can sit in whatever way is comfortable for you. If you find a lotus or half-lotus position easy, that is fine. But just as good is to sit cross-legged, or to kneel so that you sit between your legs (on a cushion if that feels better) with your calves rolled out to the sides. The most important thing is to keep your back upright and your upper body – chest, neck, shoulders and jaw – relaxed throughout.

The purpose of this meditation is to open the heart chakra to be able to feel love and compassion not just toward your immediate friends and family, but to extend the feeling further until it embraces the whole world.

LOVING MEDITATION

This meditation will help you toward compassionate understanding of all those around you — strangers as well as those you know and love, and, ultimately, even those you do not like. By appreciating that every human being, including yourself, feels pain, makes sacrifices and faces suffering, you can learn to open your heart chakra and give generous, unconditional love to all mankind. When your heart chakra is balanced, you may also find it easier to receive and accept love, calmly and serenely without insecurity or grasping.

Sit in a comfortable position with your back straight and your whole body in an alert but relaxed state. Take a few minutes to focus your mind. Close your eyes, take a long, deep breath, and slowly release it. Take another three breaths like this one. Now breathe normally, but focus your mind on your breath. As you breathe in, draw in light and energy. As you exhale, release tension and negativity.

Bring your focus to the centre of your chest, your heart chakra, and try to feel your heart as the still centre within your body as your ribs fall and rise with your breath. Each time you breathe in, draw in the kindness of the universe toward you. Each time you breathe out, send out love and gratitude in return.

Now focus on someone who has shown you kindness. In Buddhist meditation this is usually your mother. Meditate on her immeasurable kindness from when you were in the womb, through the pain of birth, to the way she cared for you constantly with unconditional love and affection. It can also be someone else who brought you up or has treated you with great kindness at some other point in your life.

See this person in your mind's eye. Now send out your love and gratitude to them as a river of golden light. Let the river flow around them so that they are encircled. Open your heart to the problems they suffer and feel how wonderful it would be if they could be relieved of suffering and be in a state of constant happiness.

Now focus on someone you barely know but see regularly. It could be the shop assistant you buy your groceries from, or the street sweeper who cleans outside your house. This person performs a service without which your life would be poorer. According to Buddhism we have lived through many lifetimes and will live through many more. Through all of these lifetimes, many kindnesses have been done for us by our fellow creatures, perhaps just as many as our own mothers have done in this lifetime.

Send your love and gratitude to this person for all they have done for you in this lifetime, in past lifetimes and lifetimes to come. Let a river of golden light encircle them with your love and kindness. Open your heart to their suffering and feel how joyous it would be if they could be relieved of all pain and be in a state of constant happiness.

Now focus on someone you do not like. This person, like you and those you love, might have physical and emotional problems. Like you, they may be afraid, confused, insecure or lonely, and they may long for peace and contentment. Any negative actions they take along their path are motivated not by you, but by their own difficulties in life.

Picture this person in your mind's eye and send out your love and compassion to them in a golden river of light that pours from your heart chakra. Let the river encircle them with your love and kindness. Open your heart to their suffering and feel how happy they would be to be relieved of all their problems so that they could achieve peace.

Now see yourself as one of an infinite number of fellow creatures, all of whom suffer and long for peace just as you do. Let a golden river of love and kindness flow from your heart chakra to embrace them all.

The Throat Chakra

Vishuddha

The throat chakra is in the hollow of the throat. Its Sanskrit name, Vishuddha, means purity or purification. As the first of the higher or universal chakras, it is responsible for your unique inner voice and communication on a spiritual level. It is also about verbal communication. A healthy throat chakra enhances self-expression and openness to the ideas of others.

The throat chakra is connected to the idea of vocation (from the Latin, *voca*, for voice) or calling. When this chakra is brought into balance, many people suddenly discover a fresh outlook on what they want to do in life. They may change their priorities or they may feel a literal vocation calling them to an entirely new profession or way of life.

About the Throat Chakra

The throat chakra is represented by a blue 16-petalled lotus at the throat. It is closely linked with the heart chakra. The throat and heart chakras should be in constant communication, processing physical, emotional and spiritual information and delivering it to all the chakras so that they work holistically.

The theme of communication is of paramount importance to the throat chakra. A closed or poorly functioning throat chakra can often be heard in a monotonous, droning voice. Using the voice and working on it in a variety of ways from using mantras to singing can help to open up the throat chakra (see pages 96–7). A healthy throat chakra ensures self-expression in every sense: being able to put forward your own ideas, while listening to the perspectives of others in an open, positive way. A closed throat chakra often means you feel defensive about your ideas, and threatened when others have different views. You may be unwilling to voice your ideas at all, preferring to align yourself to ready-made ideologies. Alternatively, you may never stop talking – but without saying anything important.

When you come to terms with your own unique inner self and its intuitions and instincts, you know this chakra is working as it should. If you are dogmatic, refuse to listen to others' advice or you get bogged down in minor details, rather than addressing the heart of an issue, you need to work on this chakra.

Giving your word is another way in which the throat chakra expresses itself. Those with strong throat chakras are reliable and mean what they say. They are able to make commitments to other people, follow a spiritual path, aspire to high ideals, and can sometimes make huge changes in their lives if they instinctively know they should. When this chakra is closed, it can leave you anxious and confused, not knowing which direction to take and fearful of taking a new path. Sometimes you can even cling to a person, an idea or a way of life even though you know it is damaging. An unhealthy throat chakra can also manifest itself in illnesses, such as neck and throat ailments, headaches, teeth and gum conditions, ear infections and mouth ulcers.

As well as doing the exercises in this chapter, you can also open the throat chakra via the written word, especially if those words express powerful ideas. Read about new religions, philosophies, cultures and lives. Read about them with an open mind; as a way of widening your understanding, tolerance and compassion, not in order to imitate or take on board wholesale someone else's view of the world.

Yoga to Open the Throat Chakra

The throat chakra governs the neck and the thyroid and parathyroid glands. Inverted yoga postures stimulate the thyroid gland – so the Shoulderstand and Plough are particularly good for opening this chakra. If you have a tendency to store tension in your neck or shoulders, do the stretches on pages 132–3 to warm-up first.

Upward-facing Dog

Known in Sanskrit as Urdhva Mukha Svanasana, this lovely arch in the back opens up the front of your chest and throat. However, if you have a bad back, just lift your body to a vertical position and don't go all the way into the arch. This pose can be quite strong on your wrists. If they ache or burn when you come out of the pose, rotate your hands in each direction for a minute or two.

Lie face down on the floor. Place your hands on the floor next to your shoulders. Breathe in and raise your whole body up, straightening your arms. Your legs should be long and straight, your toes pointed. If you can, look up to the ceiling and take five long, slow breaths.

1

Shoulderstand and Plough

These two postures, known in Sanskrit as Sarvangasana and Halasana respectively, are not only beneficial for your upper back and neck, they have many useful side-effects, such as overcoming insomnia. They can also help to relieve premenstrual syndrome and bloating. Move slowly throughout this exercise – jerky movements can damage your neck.

1 Lie on the floor on your back with your knees bent to your chest. Check there is no tension in your neck or shoulders. Breathe in and, as you breathe out, engage the uddiyana bandha (see page 54) and lift your hips off the floor, supporting them with your hands. Bring your elbows as close together as you can – this will give you better support.

2 Slowly straighten your legs. Aim to make your body and legs into one long vertical line. Place your hands in the middle of your back for support and breathe deeply, holding the position for two minutes or longer.

3 Bend your knees slightly and take them behind your head. Lower your feet gently and, if you can, put the tips of your toes on the ground. If you can, place your arms on the floor, pointing in the opposite direction to your legs. Clasp your hands. Breathe deeply in this position for two minutes or longer, pushing your legs away from you.

Camel Pose

This backward bend, Ustrasana, opens up and releases tightness and tension in your throat and neck. Avoid this posture if you have back, neck or knee problems. If you feel any discomfort in the posture, come straight out of it.

1 Kneel on the floor with your knees hip-width apart. Breathe in and, without lifting your shoulders, lift your arms above your head, engaging the mula and uddiyana bandhas (see pages 28 and 54). As you breathe out, take your right hand to your right heel. Come back up, then repeat on the left side of your body.

2 If you can, take both hands down to your heels, arching back so that you can reach them. Open up your chest and breathe slowly in this position for five breaths.

Lion Pose

This curious pose, Simhasana, is yoga for the face! It strengthens your voice and your throat.

Kneel on the floor so that you are sitting on your heels. Place your hands on your knees and check that your back is straight and your shoulders are relaxed. Breathe in and, as you breathe out, stretch out your tongue as far as it will go. As you do this, stretch your arms and fingers away from you (but keep them on your knees) and roll your eyes upward. Relax and repeat this five times.

Chi Gong Facial Massage

This chi gong facial massage is particularly good for the throat chakra. It relaxes your facial muscles where a surprising amount of tension is stored, particularly around your jaw and mouth. If you have dry or sensitive skin, apply a light coating of moisturizer before you start.

Face Washing
This massage increases the flow of blood to your face. Your face should feel warm and relaxed afterward.

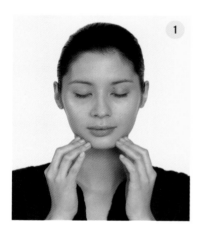

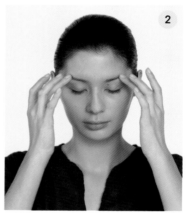

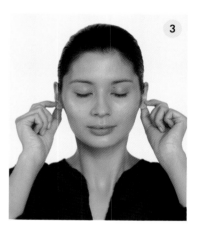

1 Place your hands so that your fingers are resting on your jawline just below your ears. Making small circles with your middle fingers, work your way gradually to the centre of your chin. Keep your jaw relaxed as you do this. Repeat three times. Now do the same movement along your jaw but using little pinches instead of circles. Repeat five times.

2 Place your middle fingers between your eyebrows and make small circles as you work your way toward your temples. Repeat several times, each time starting a fraction higher until you reach your hairline.

3 Hold your earlobes between your thumbs and forefingers. Gently rub the lobes. Now work your way along the outer edge of the ears, gently rubbing all the way until you reach the tops. Repeat five times.

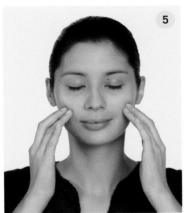

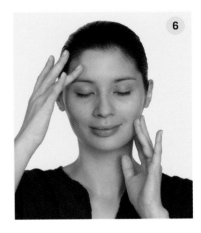

4 To stimulate your eye area, begin with your middle fingers on the inner corners of each eyebrow. Now, making little tapping movements as you go, work your way along your eyebrows, then follow the eye sockets round, across to the top of your cheekbones and up the sides of your nose. Circle your eyes five times. Then starting again at the inner corners of your eyebrows, squeeze along their whole length using your thumbs and forefingers. Move to your temples and, using your forefingers and middle fingers, rub in gentle circles. Repeat five times.

5 Starting at the base of your nose, press the three middle fingers of each hand below your cheekbones, gradually working out in a line toward your ears. Repeat several times, each time beginning a fraction lower until you reach the jawline.

6 Use all your fingers to pat your face gently in a ripple effect tracing the outline of your face from your forehead, out past your ears to your jawline and into the centre of your chin. Then let your fingers play over the whole of your face in a random gentle tapping movement for two minutes.

Balancing the Throat Chakra

The throat chakra is associated with the mouth, speech and communication. It governs not just your throat, but your neck, lungs, jaw and vocal chords. These areas – particularly your neck and jaw – commonly store tension and can become stiff and immobile, leading to headaches, migraines and backache. The following exercises and breathing techniques are designed to help you find your voice, and/or to release tension from the area of your throat chakra so that energy can flow more freely. This, in turn, enables you to open yourself to pure expression. Do all of these exercises slowly and smoothly.

The throat chakra is the first of the universal or spiritual chakras – before you work on it, it is important to bring the previous four chakras into balance. Practise the fasting, water cleansing and breathing exercises of the preceding chapters before you start work on the throat chakra.

Finding Your Voice
Using your voice is one of the best ways to develop the throat chakra, especially if you tend to be quiet or reserved. Many people believe that they just can't sing or they don't have a voice – it's more likely to be the case that they've mislaid their voice or never found it. Start by simply humming a tune to yourself and try to let your throat and neck muscles relax. You don't have to make a great deal of noise – just try to hear the tune inside your head and feel the music vibrating in your throat. Let go of your inhibitions. Try not to be critical of the way you sound.

When you feel comfortable, try singing out loud. This is something that people reputedly do in the bath, but you can sing at any time – while you are driving to work, gardening or doing housework, for example. Singing out loud is profoundly liberating. We can store a great deal of tension in the throat, the neck and the voice itself – not just physical tension but emotional tension too. As a result, singing can be an exhilarating experience. Some people actually feel the throat chakra open up when they sing and become much more aware of it as a centre. This experience may feel like a sensation of intense joy (or a bubbling liquid in the throat) at moments of great emotion or awareness. Reciting the sacred syllable "om" (see page 96) is another good way to find your voice.

Crystal Meditation
The throat chakra is represented by a range of blue colours, from light sky blue to the

RELEASING UPPER BODY TENSION

These three exercises help you to get rid of the tension in your shoulders, neck, mouth and jaw. Do the first two exercises in front of a mirror so that you can check whether your shoulders are relaxed and level at the beginning of the first exercise and at the end of the second.

Head Rolls and Turns

Stand up straight, with relaxed shoulders, your arms by your sides and your feet hip-width apart. Look in the mirror to check that your shoulders are level and dropped, and there is no tension in your face. Shift your jaw from side to side and open your mouth wide, then let all your facial muscles relax and let your mouth close.

Drop your chin to your chest and feel the stretch up the back of your neck. Relax into this position for a few breaths.

Without moving your shoulders, roll your head toward your right shoulder. Then take your head back to the centre and roll it to the left. Alternate sides, stretching your neck as far as it will go. Do this four times on each side.

Lift your head so that you are looking straight ahead and then turn it as far as it will go to look over your right shoulder. Hold for a moment and then turn to look over your left shoulder. Repeat, moving slowly and without tension, four times on each side.

Shoulder Circles and Drops

Stand as before with your shoulders relaxed and your arms hanging loosely at your sides. Roll your shoulders forward toward your chest. Keep your arms relaxed – they will move of their own accord.

Lift your shoulders up toward your ears and then roll them back so that you gently squeeze your shoulder blades together. Lower them into their normal position. Repeat this circling movement three more times, then reverse the direction for another four circles.

Now lift your shoulders up as high as you can toward your ears, then let them drop. Let go of tension as you do this. Look in the mirror to check that your shoulders are level and relaxed after each drop. Repeat this four times.

Opening the Upper Body

Sit on a chair so that your knees are bent at right angles to your thighs with your feet flat on the floor. Keep your back long and straight, your shoulders relaxed and your head held high. Focus straight ahead and let your arms hang by your sides. Draw your navel to your spine as you breathe out.

Breathe in and raise your arms so that they are folded loosely, level with your breastbone. Your hands should be relaxed rather than gripping your arms. Breathe out and start to turn from your waist toward the right.

Turn as far as you can to the right, leading with your right elbow and making sure that the turn comes from your waist only. Your head follows the movement rather than leads it. Your hips should stay absolutely still. When you have turned as far as you can, breathe in and return to the centre. Repeat on the left side, then alternate, turning 10 times in each direction.

deep blue of lapis lazuli. If you're not sure what this colour looks like, you see it most often, and to greatest effect, in medieval books of hours and medieval stained glass windows, both of which use pigments made from the lapis lazuli stone. This is a colour that has enormous resonance in the mind – if you see it in a dream, you will remember it when you awake.

Use a piece of lapis lazuli when you are meditating: simply place a piece near you so that you can see it through half-closed eyes. Alternatively, use other blue stones, such as blue quartz, turquoise or sodalite.

The Throat Lock

The throat lock, jalandhara bandha, is the third of the three yogic locks (for the other two, see pages 28 and 54) that promote the flow of both prana (life-force) and kundalini energy. You can engage jalandhara bandha by simultaneously exhaling through your nose, making a noise, and dropping your chin to your chest. You will feel your throat lock. When jalandhara bandha is closed it prevents the escape of prana. Be aware of jalandhara bandha when you do Shoulderstand and Plough earlier in this chapter (see page 87).

THE ART OF LISTENING

Although the throat chakra is most closely associated with the voice and self-expression, listening is just as important. Listening is the flip side of the coin of communication. When you are in conversation, listen very carefully to what the other person is saying: don't interrupt or go off at tangents. Make sure that when you respond, your response accurately reflects what you have heard and is both well-considered and well-expressed.

Most of us have lost the art of listening properly. But there are a number of ways to regain this skill. One delightful way is to listen to stories. You can find everything from children's stories to literary classics recorded on tape or CD. Some stories are read by a single narrator, others by an entire cast of actors playing different roles. When a story is well-narrated or acted, the development of plot and character can be a richly stimulating experience and one that brings cosy memories of bedtime stories flooding back. This kind of listening is a completely different experience from watching the same story on television or at the cinema. In the absence of pictures, your imagination fills in the gaps and you start to play an active role in the story. There are also an increasing number of professional story-tellers around. They work in a diverse range of venues from libraries to art centres and theatres – you can find them on the internet.

You can also listen to music, of course. Even if you don't think it's your thing, try listening to classical music – there are plenty of classical music radio stations that you can explore. The reason I suggest classical music is threefold. First, it offers the opportunity to focus on the sound of the music rather than the meaning of the words. Second, it is complex, so you have to listen really hard! Third, it has been found that listening to classical music (and no other kind) stimulates and harmonizes the brain waves.

Good Vibrations

There are a number of instruments, such as Tibetan "singing bowls" and cymbals, that create sound that vibrates and changes in a long, drawn-out way. You can buy them at esoteric shops and they are made of an alloy of a number of metals. Their quality (and price) varies with the quality of the metals. The effect of listening to these instruments is not dissimilar to that of chanting, using the "om" mantra (see page 96) or practising Brahmari breathing (see box, opposite).

YOGIC BREATHING EXERCISES

Brahmari Breathing

This is a special form of yogic breathing in which you make a sound on both your inhalation and your exhalation. You may find it a bit odd or amusing at first, but it is said to develop a beautiful voice.

1 Sit with crossed legs and a straight back, supported if necessary. Inhale through your nose, while closing your glottis (voice box) so that you make a soft snoring sound. Hold your breath for as long as possible.

2 Breathe out slowly while humming. Try to extend the exhalation for as long as possible. Repeat five to ten times.

Sitkari Breathing

This exercise and the one that follows are unusual in yogic breathing in that you inhale through your mouth rather than through your nose. Both exercises have a cooling effect on your body and relieve feelings of hunger and thirst.

1 Sit as for Brahmari breathing. Slowly inhale through your mouth with the tip of your tongue pressed against your upper palate. Make a slight hissing sound. Hold your breath for as long as possible.

2 Exhale slowly and fully through your nose. Repeat five to ten times.

Sithali Breathing

This is a good exercise to practise when you are feeling hot and uncomfortable. If you are unable to roll your tongue, do the previous exercise instead.

1 Sit as for Brahmari breathing. Curl the sides of your tongue up and stick the end of your tongue out slightly. Breathe in, drawing the air through the tube formed by your curled tongue. Close your mouth and hold your breath for as long as you can.

2 Exhale slowly and fully through your nose. Repeat five to ten times.

Expressing Yourself

Many people assume that the heart chakra is the seat of all emotion. In fact, the throat chakra is just as crucial because it governs the expression of our thoughts and feelings. Without this self-expression, we not only limit the openness of our hearts, we may fail to understand what we really feel or think.

When you feel troubled and confused about something, take a piece of paper and write down all your thoughts, ideas and feelings about this issue. Be as honest as you can – if you feel self-conscious, remind yourself that this is for your eyes only. Look at the problem from every possible angle and point of view. When you have written down everything you can think of, put the piece of paper to one side and do a short meditation, such as the mantra meditation on page 97. Then return to your piece of paper – read what you have written calmly and objectively, and see if you have a new perspective or insight into your problem and how to deal with it.

Externalizing a problem by writing it down – providing you do it calmly, without anger or fear – can often bring new understanding and insight.

As well as expressing confusing or negative thoughts, it is healthy to express positive ones. The expression of positive thoughts and feelings resonates with others and spreads happiness. It is good to feel love, and it is vital to tell your loved ones how you feel – for both you and them.

Throat Chakra Meditation

This meditation opens and stimulates the throat chakra. It is based on the sound of your voice reciting a mantra. This can be extremely liberating, especially if you are not particularly vocal. Many people are surprised how much tension they usually hold in their throat and voice.

Mantras have been used for thousands of years in the East as a tool for meditation. When I spent some time in a Buddhist monastery, we used both mantras and chanting, notably in evening sessions when they were very joyful and releasing, especially after a day of silence. The chanting usually consisted of prayers sung to a simple tune. A mantra can be defined as a single sound repeated over and over again, either silently in your mind or in a quiet singing voice. All mantras, however they are used, are a means to focus the mind to a single point of concentration. In this meditation you say the mantra aloud to benefit the throat chakra.

If you learn meditation in a monastery or from a teacher, you may be given your own mantra to recite. Alternatively, or in the absence of a personal teacher, you can choose one yourself. It can be a word that has special significance for you, such as "peace", or one that produces a resonant sound. The best-known of these is "om" – the sacred sound of the universe; the vibrational tone of the ultimate reality. It is actually a much longer, drawn-out sound than the word suggests – you should make the sound "a" on a long, slow exhalation followed by "o", then "u" and finally the humming "m" sound, which you should hold for as long as possible. The aim is to reach a stage where the sound and its resonance fills your entire mind and body.

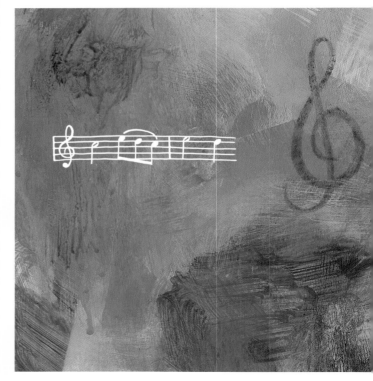

MANTRA MEDITATION

Using your voice to sing, hum or chant is a powerful tool for opening the heart chakra. Whether you choose to chant "om" or to recite your own personal mantra in the following meditation, focus on letting the sound fill your entire body and consciousness. Begin to make your chosen sound as you start to breathe out, and aim to prolong the sound and the exhalation for as long as possible. You can chant your mantra softly if you wish, or you can vary the volume from loud to quiet during the meditation session.

Sit in a comfortable position with a long, straight back (on a chair, if necessary). Make sure that your shoulders are relaxed and hold your hands in your lap with your palms facing upward, your right hand on top of your left. Your hands should be soft, your fingers slightly curled and your thumbs touching. Don't press your arms against your sides, just let them relax, slightly away from your body.

Check that your jaw is relaxed with your teeth slightly apart. Relax your mouth and lips, and let your tongue rest against your upper teeth. Bend your head slightly so that your gaze rests on the floor in front of you. Almost close your eyes or, if you find it too distracting to have any visual stimulus, close them completely.

Begin by settling your mind and focusing on your breath. Take three long, slow, deep breaths in through your nose and out through your mouth. Visualize the passage of air bringing cleansing, life-giving oxygen to your body and the exhalation of air removing distraction and negativity along with carbon dioxide.

On your next inhalation, feel your breath fill your body and mind and then, as you very slowly exhale, sound out the mantra that you have chosen. If you are using "om" — a particularly strong mantra owing to the nature of its sound — make sure that you pronounce each of the four sounds separately and finish with the "m" as a humming sound for as long as you can. This should be the longest of each of the four sounds. Feel your chosen sound vibrating through your whole body and mind. Keep reciting your mantra for five to ten minutes (in time you can build up to 20 minutes).

After you have recited the final mantra, slowly bring your consciousness back to your breath, allowing the sound of the mantra and its vibration through your body to fade gently into the background. Return to breathing normally, and gradually become aware of your surroundings. Don't get up straight away — allow yourself a little time to enjoy the peaceful afterglow of the meditation before you return to your normal routine.

The Brow Chakra

Ajna

The brow chakra is situated at the point of your third eye in the centre of your forehead between your eyes and above your nose. The third eye looks beyond ordinary vision and toward transcendence, divine purpose and spiritual awareness.

The brow chakra is associated with the brain, and when this chakra is in balance, you can exhibit extraordinary clarity of thought, combining logical reasoning with intuition and inspiration. The brow chakra strives for completeness in terms of the self — an inner harmony between body, mind and spirit — and in terms of the divine, the creator or the whole of creation itself.

About the Brow Chakra

The Sanskrit name for this chakra is Ajna, which has a twin meaning of both perception and command. Perception here includes not just perception of others and the world, but also self-realization – the ability to see yourself with honesty and insight – and perception of the divine or spiritual.

As with any spiritual development, opening the brow chakra requires a level of intense honesty with both yourself and others. Unflinching honesty can make your life – and others' lives – quite uncomfortable at times. When the brow chakra is open and balanced, it accepts no excuses. So, however difficult a choice may be, if the brow chakra knows it is the right one, you are compelled to follow that path. Responding with "I can't", or absolving yourself from responsibility by blaming your past or other people for things, simply won't work. The brow chakra has the ability to command you to do something.

Because the brow chakra can make our lives so uncomfortable, most people find it easier to close it down. This, on the surface at least, makes life a lot less testing. You don't need to worry about the path you're taking in life or about the effects of your words and actions on others. It is a state of being that is the very opposite of the Buddhist concept of mindfulness, in which you must examine the motivation behind every thought, word and deed.

However, closing down the brow chakra doesn't bring peace and freedom from worry or bother; it means an end to perception and discernment. When you close down the brow chakra, you become a poor judge of people and situations, finding yourself in a series of muddles and poor choices – or worse. You lose a sense of purpose and become so self-absorbed that your relationships become dysfunctional.

So, although balancing the brow chakra may be hard work, it is clearly worth it. This is certainly true for those who wish for spiritual development. And that spark of inspiration that is ignited by opening the brow chakra exists in all of us. In people with a blocked brow chakra, inspiration can be subverted into fantasy or into an activity such as watching television all day. In people whose brow chakra is too open (which can result from taking mind-expanding drugs or belonging to a misguided cult), nightmares, disturbed and uncontrollable thought patterns and even hallucinations can result. When the brow chakra's energy is strong, inspiration takes many positive forms: from flashes of intuition to sudden insights about how to solve a problem; from a sense of the divine in all things to moments of pure clairvoyance.

Yoga to Stimulate the Brow Chakra

The yoga postures for the brow chakra emphasize focus, concentration and balance. The better your focus – both mental and visual – the more able you will be to hold a posture for extended periods. The direction of your eyes and the steadiness of your gaze directly affect your ability to balance.

Eagle Pose

This pose, Garudasana, leads your focus directly toward the brow chakra. It looks like a complicated posture, but is actually a relaxing stretch for your upper back as well as a still balance. The eagle, incidentally, represents the power of the spirit.

Stand in a stable posture, with your feet hip-width apart and your arms at your sides. Breathe deeply for a few moments and focus on becoming very still. Breathe in and, as you breathe out, bend your knees without lifting your heels and cross your left leg over your right, with your toes behind your right calf. On your next out-breath, cross your right arm over your left, bend your elbows and bring your palms as close together as you can, fingers pointing upward (one hand will always be higher than the other). Lift your elbows as high as you can without lifting your shoulders. Focus on your brow chakra. Hold this position for at least a minute, then cross your arms and legs in the other direction.

Cobra

This elegant back bend, Bhujangasana, stimulates your brain and nervous system, both of which are governed by the brow chakra. The strength you need to rise off the floor should come from your abdominal muscles rather than from your shoulders and back, but if you have back problems, don't rise too high.

1 Lie face down on the floor with your hands immediately below your shoulders. Place your legs together, feet pointed. Draw your shoulder blades down into your back. Breathe in and, as you breathe out, rise smoothly off the floor, head first, using your abdominal and back muscles. Don't push up using your hands. In fact, to check you are using the correct muscles, take your hands off the floor.

2 Put your hands back on the floor and continue to rise until your arms start to straighten. Keep your shoulders down. Check that your legs are still together and there is no tension in your shoulders. Take five long, slow breaths in this position and then relax.

Headstand

The Headstand, or Sirsasana, is one of the most important poses in yoga and is especially stimulating for the brow chakra, the brain and the nervous system. It is also ultimately relaxing and good for insomnia. You may want to start by trying to do the Headstand against a wall. Eventually, your aim is to be free-standing, but the presence of a wall often helps to build confidence when you are learning the posture. Do not do this posture if you have a back or neck injury. Women should avoid inverted postures such as Headstand when they are menstruating.

1 Kneel down and place your arms on the floor, clasping your elbows in your hands. Without moving your elbows, open your forearms and link your fingers together in front of you. Rest the back of your head against your forearms. Straighten your legs and walk your feet toward your head so that your back is vertical.

2 When you have walked your feet as close to your head as you can, engage your abdominal muscles and bend your knees and lift your legs gently upward. Take five long, slow breaths in this position.

Child's Pose

After the exertions of the Headstand, Child's Pose, Balasana, is the ideal way to relax. If you prefer, you can place a cushion under your forehead, or turn your face to one side – although turn it both ways to achieve balance.

Kneel on the floor and sit back on your heels. Gently fold over your knees, resting your forehead on the floor and placing your arms next to your body. Your hands should be close to your feet, palms facing up. Breathe gently and try to let all your muscles relax.

3 When you feel ready, straighten your legs and take five long, slow breaths, or more if you feel comfortable. Come down slowly and rest in the posture that follows next: Child's Pose.

Chi Gong to Stimulate the Brow Chakra

These two chi gong exercises involve lifting your arms and with them, your focus and consciousness. Practise the correct way to lift your arms high first – if you lift your shoulders as well, this brings tension into the movement.

Lifting the Sky
Make the movements strong and slow in this exercise, stretching and straightening your arms as far as they will go.

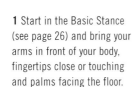
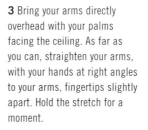

1 Start in the Basic Stance (see page 26) and bring your arms in front of your body, fingertips close or touching and palms facing the floor.

2 Start to raise your arms out to the sides in a wide circle.

3 Bring your arms directly overhead with your palms facing the ceiling. As far as you can, straighten your arms, with your hands at right angles to your arms, fingertips slightly apart. Hold the stretch for a moment.

4 Lower your arms until your hands are just above your head. Bring your arms back to the starting position and repeat the movement up to 20 times.

LIFTING YOUR ARMS CORRECTLY

Always lift your arms from the centre of your back rather than by raising your shoulders. It helps to practise in front of a mirror so you can actually see if your shoulders move. Relax your shoulders by doing some shoulder circles and drops (see page 93). Then place the back of one hand on the opposite shoulder blade. Now raise your free arm first to the front and then to the side, keeping the shoulder itself lowered throughout. As you start to move, you will feel the working shoulder blade move in and down. If you tend to lift your shoulder along with your arm, you will detect this from the way your shoulder blade moves. Learning to move your arms while keeping your shoulders relaxed, will improve your posture and make neck problems or tension headaches less likely.

Plucking Stars

The hand changes may seem a bit of a brain teaser at first, but once you have worked them out, make the movements as slow and fluid as possible.

1

2

3

4

1 Stand in the Basic Stance (see page 26). Hold your arms in front of you, elbows bent, your left arm level with your abdomen, your right arm level with your chest, palms facing each other as if you were holding a beach ball.

2 Lift your left hand upward so that it passes your right hand.

3 When your left hand is near your face, turn the palm to face the sky and continue to push upward. At the same time push your right hand down toward the ground.

4 Keep pushing until both arms are straight. Keep your fingers pointing inward. Bring your arms back to the starting position, but the opposite way round. Repeat the movement. Continue alternating arms up to 10 times.

Balancing the Brow Chakra

Bringing the brow chakra into balance creates a sense of inner peace, stillness and harmony. It is very much about opening the mind to the divine and the spiritual, and there are a number of ways of encouraging this to happen.

The brow chakra has a strong urge toward a sense of completion and being at one with the rest of creation. Good ways to open and balance the brow chakra include finding a place of quiet and solitude within nature, contemplating natural beauty or practising meditation, yoga or chi gong outdoors in a beautiful place. If you can't be in natural surroundings easily, buy a tape of birdsong or other natural sounds, fill your home with scented flowers (hyacinths have a particularly stimulating effect on the brow chakra), or use incense or fragrances that stimulate this chakra, such as rose or geranium.

Create an Affirmation

Affirmations are simple, positive statements of intent. They can help to keep you focused on what you want to achieve in life. Over time, they can help you to change old negative ways of thinking into positive ones. Balancing the brow chakra has the ability to change the way you view your life and your purpose. You just have to overcome the fear of success to allow the affirmations to succeed. Affirmations can be repeated either verbally or in your mind.

Think or say them slowly and firmly 20 times or write them out 50 times each day in a journal that you keep just for this purpose. Keep your attention firmly on the affirmations as you think, say or write them. You can also meditate on an affirmation. The following are simply suggestions for affirmations. If you feel there is a particular area of your life that needs to open up to third-eye energy, create your own affirmation.

If you lead a hectic life that seems to leave no time for peace or meditation, your affirmation could be: "I allow stillness and silence into my life."

If you find it difficult to embrace the idea that you can be guided by intuition, your affirmation could be: "I allow my divine inner self to guide me."

If you feel confused about relationships, work or any other problem, your affirmation could be: "My inner wisdom guides me to my true path."

Accept Your Intuition

The brow chakra is the seat of discernment. This doesn't just mean perceiving the moral or spiritual path that is right for

GOING ON A RETREAT

To truly concentrate on opening the brow chakra and developing your spiritual practice, you need to find a place of peace and solitude, especially one where you will be given spiritual guidance. The ideal place for such peace and spiritual practice is a retreat. This may seem like a huge commitment, but there are many different kinds of retreats: some last for several weeks, but others last for a weekend or a day. Still others offer a place for meditation or contemplation for just an hour or two.

The majority of retreats are attached to religious institutions, mainly Christian or Buddhist. There are also mind-body-spirit centres that have no affiliation to a religion, but rather to their own spiritual approach. My longest retreat was for a month at a Buddhist monastery in the Nepalese Himalaya, although the teaching was by Tibetan monks and lamas. This entailed daily teachings on the principles of Buddhism by the lama, several different kinds of daily meditation, discussions of the teachings with the monks, as well as a certain amount of fasting and silence. The name of the course was the Lam Rim, meaning The Graduated Path to Enlightenment. It was a powerful course – with many deeply uncomfortable brow-chakra opening moments of self-realization. And it gave a profound insight into the Buddhist concept of mindfulness – making sure that everything you think or do is done with the right motivation and not from the Buddhist engenderers of suffering – anger, attachment or ignorance.

You can find a retreat to suit you closer to home and for a much shorter period. Many Catholic and Anglican monasteries and Quaker centres run retreats. Some retreats encompass the physical as well as the spiritual: try a yoga retreat, or going to a mind-body-spirit centre that offers a variety of healing and spiritual development techniques. Guidebooks are available that list retreats.

you on a logical, rational level. This chakra also gives you sudden and profound insights, moments of intuition and inspiration when you suddenly see things clearly and realise what you must do. Unfortunately, in our materialistic times, this capacity for insight is often mistrusted and underrated and, as a consequence, the brow chakra becomes dormant or closed. However, as you work on this chakra, you may start to intuit answers to life's questions on every level, from spiritual development to changing your job.

In the Tibetan Buddhist tradition, these intuitions are known as realisations. You can spend weeks, months or years grappling with a problem or concept but there is a moment when you suddenly *know*. Don't ignore realisations – they are the voice of your brow chakra.

TRATAK

Tratak is a yogic concentration exercise that naturally stills the mind and prepares it for a deeper level of concentration and ultimately meditation. It entails gazing at an object or a focus point without blinking, and then closing your eyes to visualize your chosen object. This is an ideal exercise for increasing single-pointed concentration, for steadying a wandering mind and also for visualizing the brow chakra. In yoga it is one of six purification practices, known as kriyas, and it is believed to purify the mind, stimulate the brain and improve the eyesight.

1 Choose a place to practise tratak. Given the brow chakra's affinity with nature and beauty, the perfect place is in natural surroundings. If you are lucky enough to be able to use a mountain, a lake or a tree in the exercise, this is ideal. At night you could use the moon or a star to focus upon. If you practise indoors, you might like to choose a beautiful flower, a candle flame or a crystal. Alternatively, there may be a statue or a simple picture (anything too complex encourages your thoughts to run away) that appeals to you. When you have chosen a place that feels right, sit in a comfortable position with a long, straight spine so that the object you are going to focus on is at eye level.

2 Begin by focusing on your breath. Take a long slow in-breath to the count of five. Hold your breath for a count of five. Then exhale completely for five counts. Repeat this three times. Check that your body is completely relaxed, especially your neck, shoulders and back.

Finally, check there is no tension in your face muscles, particularly around your jaw.

3 Allow your breathing to return to normal and take your focus to your chosen object. Gaze at it steadily without blinking. Your eyes may begin to water. After about a minute, gently close your eyes and visualize the object exactly as it was, but seeing it through the third eye of the brow chakra rather than your eyes.

4 When you can no longer hold the image in your third eye, open your eyes and gaze at it again unblinkingly. When you can no longer continue to gaze, or your eyes begin to water, close them and visualize the object again through the third eye. Repeat this for several minutes, gradually extending the gazing time with each practice. Over time you will be able to hold your focus for longer periods, and from this you can move seamlessly into meditation.

RELEASING TENSION FROM YOUR EYES

These two exercises release tension that is stored in your eyes and head. This, in turn, helps to relieve stress that is stored in your mind. It may help to do the neck, head and shoulder stretches on page 93 first.

Eye Exercises

Most of the time, we turn our heads to look at something, rather than use our gaze to its full extent. These simple eye movements strengthen the muscles in your eyes, help to prevent headaches and eye strain, and may improve vision.

Sit on a chair with your feet flat on the ground, or sit cross-legged on the floor. Your neck should be in line with the rest of your spine.

Without moving your head or engaging your facial muscles, look up as high and as low as you can. Hold your gaze in each position and repeat the movement five times.

Now look as far as you can to the right, holding the gaze, and then to the left. Repeat five times on each side.

Move your eyes diagonally from high right to low left and then high left to low right. Do each movement five times.

Circle your gaze twice in one direction, then twice in the other.

Palming

This is a lovely way of soothing the eyes after the muscular exertions of the previous exercise.

Sit in the same position as for the previous exercise and check that there is no tension in your body. Rub your palms together vigorously for a few moments until they start to feel warm. Place them over your closed eyes so that they form a cup to keep out the light. Don't press on your eyes. Enjoy the warmth and darkness, and let any tension go from your eyes.

Brow Chakra Meditation

The brow chakra needs calm and serenity if it is to function properly and open your mind to inspiration and intellectual and spiritual wisdom. Stress and mental overload can cause imbalance in the brow chakra, and this imbalance may cause migraine headaches, terrifying nightmares and mental exhaustion. It may also cause problems that affect your eyes – either in the form of allergies or problems with your vision. This meditation uses the visualization of a beautiful garden to bring your brow chakra into balance.

The brow chakra governs your mind, both its intellectual power and its search for spiritual knowledge. It is through the brow chakra, too, that you can contemplate beauty. The meditation opposite aims to develop all of these areas, and is also a way to sharpen your focus and improve your memory. Unlike the single-pointed concentration facilitated by an exercise such as tratak (see page 110), this meditation involves focusing on more than one thing and is described as a category meditation. If your mind tends to wander during other forms of meditation, you may find this one helpful.

I've used the image of a garden and various plants in the meditation. Feel free to vary the plants or completely change the location. The important thing is to keep the four categories (strength, beauty, tranquillity and nourishment) and to explore and focus on each one in turn, and then to bring the four parts together and integrate them in your mind.

CATEGORY MEDITATION

Sit in a comfortable position on a chair or on the floor with your back straight and supported. Check that your neck is in line with your spine and that your chin is tilted slightly downward. Make sure that you are not holding any tension in your shoulders, neck or back.

Close your eyes and spend a little time settling yourself. Take a deep breath in, drawing in calmness and tranquillity as you do so. As you breathe out, let go of any persistent thoughts and anxieties. Take three breaths in this way.

Visualize yourself sitting in a lovely garden. The garden is grassy and you are sitting in its very centre. Enjoy the feeling of the earth beneath you, giving you centring energy and calming your mind. In each corner of the garden, there is something different. In the left corner in front of you is a weeping willow. See how its graceful branches arch and trail to the ground. Look at the delicate green of each leaf as it is blown by a gentle breeze. In your mind's eye explore the willow from the shape of its boughs to each tiny leaf. See the roots beneath the earth, drawing up the earth's energy just as you are. Visualize the tiniest details of the tree, absorb the tree's strength into you and then return your focus to the centre of the garden where you sit, still and unmoving.

Now focus on the right-hand corner in front of you where there is a beautiful rambling rose, climbing over the wall. Explore the rose. What colour are its flowers? Are they open to the sun? Are there buds that are closed? Do the flowers still have morning dew on them? How high does the rose ramble? Does it spread wide across the wall? Is the wall made of brick or stone, or is it a wooden fence? Look more closely at the flowers. Are the petals as soft as velvet or do they have a brilliant glossy sheen? Are there bees buzzing and gently sipping nectar? Visualize the rose in its entirety and in the smallest detail. Absorb its beauty into yourself and return your focus to the centre of the garden where you sit, still and unmoving.

Behind your right shoulder is a fountain. You do not need to turn to see it because you can hear the playing of the water. Visualize the fountain. Is it grand with a great tower of water shooting into the air? Or is it a small fountain with its water splashing over pebbles? Is it on the ground, in a surrounding pool, on a pedestal, or pouring out of a fountainhead on a wall into a pool below? Are there birds coming to drink? Does the fountain splash the surrounding plants and grass with its life-giving water? Visualize your fountain in its entirety and in detail, and absorb its tranquillity into yourself. Return your focus to the centre of the garden where you sit still and unmoving.

Behind your left shoulder is a fruit tree. You don't need to turn to see it, because you can smell the scent of the fruit ripening in the sun. What sort of tree is it? Does it have apples, pears, cherries hanging from its boughs? Is it an orange or a lemon tree? Does it have the heady scent of an exotic fruit such as mango or papaya? Visualize the fruit as ripe and juicy – ready to pick and eat. Does the tree give shade to the surrounding garden? Are there birds or animals, such as squirrels or even monkeys, feasting on its fruit? Visualize the fruit. See the sheen or the down of its skin. Visualize the sweet interior of the fruit. See the seed at its core, promising more life and more fruit. Visualize the fruit and the tree and absorb its nourishing sweetness inside yourself.

Return your focus to the centre of the garden where you sit, still and unmoving. See the whole garden around you – the three plants and the fountain – and feel what they have given you. Visualize how you have absorbed their strength, beauty, tranquillity and nourishing sweetness. Be aware of how whole this makes you feel, and how much stronger and how much more supported you are. Enjoy this feeling for as long as you wish and then slowly bring your focus back to where you are sitting in your room.

The Crown Chakra

Sahasrara

The seventh and final chakra is the crown chakra, or Sahasrara, which means both one thousand and infinity. This chakra represents knowing your true path and living your life accordingly. It is far removed from the root chakra's will to survive. Some people describe the opening of the crown chakra as a surrender to the divine will, or being as one with the universe. The ego withers and is replaced by a universal consciousness.

The symbol of the crown chakra is the thousand-petalled lotus, often shown floating above the head like a halo. When the seventh chakra is in balance, you experience peace and fulfilment. While such moments are rare and transitory, being entirely in the crown chakra offers glimpses of enlightenment and bliss.

About the Crown Chakra

Opening the crown chakra is the final stage in the development begun by the previous two chakras – the throat and the brow chakra. If the brow chakra's aim is toward fulfilment and purpose, it is at the crown chakra that you truly achieve this.

The crown chakra sees life entirely from a spiritual perspective. When it is closed or blocked, there is a refusal to engage in or even believe in the spiritual. This is often the case for people who argue that there is nothing beyond what the five senses can perceive, the material world and the will of the ego. This rationalist argument persuades that everything can be explained mundanely; that there is no soul or spirituality, just the ego, and fantasy or whimsy. This complete denial of seventh chakra reality often leads to arrogance and materialism and, when life deals out sudden changes, its adherents are often left unable to cope, lacking any underlying meaning to their lives.

Because the crown chakra gives life meaning, your life generally takes a completely new direction when you bring this chakra into balance. And that direction comes from a new sense of purpose: the purpose of life and of your soul. By honouring your true self, you love and honour the rest of creation. This self is not to be confused with the ego. The seventh chakra sees through the delusions of the ego and views them and the rest of life with a certain detachment. It creates an inner calm that often draws others to you.

The crown chakra is on the top of the head. In newborn babies, this spot is called the fontanelle or the soft spot – it is the place where the bones of the skull have not yet fused together. In visualizations, you can reopen this spot to allow light, the divine spirit and inspiration to pour into you. By opening yourself up to the spirit of creation, you learn your true purpose, you receive guidance on your spiritual path and you are able to recognize soulmates. Often you see the world through new eyes, viewing it with a sense of wonder that you last knew when you were a child.

The seventh chakra embraces both the Christian concept of loving your neighbour as yourself and the Buddhist detachment that sees the material world as an illusion: "samsara". It is, of course, far easier to block this knowledge which lies deep within us all and continue with a smaller, less demanding life – and most of us do. But, whether we recognize it or not, we all yearn for oneness with the divine and, through the crown chakra, we may sometimes make that ultimate connection.

Yoga for Contemplation

Because the crown chakra is a spiritual portal rather than a physical one, it may seem strange to suggest physical postures in order to access it. However, the postures that follow are all ideal for use with meditation and contemplation.

Tree Pose

This posture, known in Sanskrit as Vrksasana, links the crown and root chakras, and is both rooting and uplifting. Focus on stilling your body.

Stand with your feet hip-width apart and your arms at your sides. Breathe deeply for a few moments to focus your concentration. Lift your left knee and press it up toward your chest with your hands, then take it out to the side and place your left foot against your right thigh as high up your right leg as you can. Bring your hands together in prayer position at chest height and keep pressing your left leg back to open up the position. Breathe five long, deep breaths (or more if you can) and then release the pose and repeat on the other side of your body.

Half-lotus

Although you can meditate in any position you choose, this and the Full-lotus (Padmasana) are the classic poses for meditation. Try to alternate legs – the pose will inevitably be easier on one side than the other. As you become more supple, you may want to try the Full-lotus.

Sit up with a long, straight back, against a wall if this helps. Bend your right leg at the knee so that your right foot rests against your left inner thigh. Take your left foot and place it on your right thigh, as close as you can to your right hip without straining. Your left knee will probably be off the floor and you can place a support, such as a cushion, beneath it. If you find the position very difficult, you can make it easier by sitting on a block or a folded blanket. Close your eyes and breathe for five long, deep breaths (or more) and repeat the pose on the other side. To do a Full-lotus, take the foot that is on the floor and place it as close to the opposite hip socket as you can.

Reclining Hero

Reclining Hero, or Supta Virasana, is a strong posture and a strong stretch, but when you become comfortable in it, it is a good posture in which to meditate. If you have tight thigh muscles, go only as far as is comfortable and sit on a thick book (or books) to make the posture easier. Never strain or force your muscles. If you feel discomfort, release the pose straight away.

1 Sit on the floor or on a thick book with your knees slightly apart and your calves open. Take a long, deep breath and, as you exhale, feel your spine lengthen.

2 Start to lean back, placing your hands on the floor behind you for support. If you feel any strain, stop here. If not, keep going and try to place your elbows on the floor. You will need to tilt your pelvis upward to avoid arching in your back.

3 If you are still not straining, try to lower your back down onto the floor. If you are using a book or books to make you comfortable in this pose, don't attempt this step. Try to keep your knees together and stretch your arms out above your head. It is important to keep tilting your pelvis upward in this position. Try to relax your thighs. Get to the position you feel most comfortable in, then stop and take five long, deep breaths.

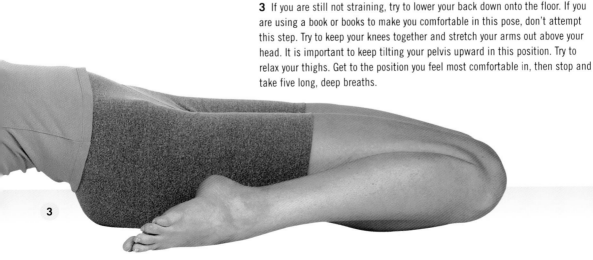

Preparing Yourself for Meditation

These two simple exercises help to turn your concentration inward and give you the alertness and focus that you need for meditation.

Calming Chi

This quietening exercise is from chi gong. It reconnects the crown and root chakras and is a good way to end any chi gong session and to prepare for meditation.

1 Stand in the Basic Stance (see page 26) with your hands at navel level, palms facing downward.

2 Breathe in and slowly raise your hands in front of your body.

3 Raise your palms to face level and turn them to face you. Rise onto tiptoes. Breathe out, lower your heels, bend your knees and lower your arms. Do the exercise up to 10 times, then put your hands on your belly and take 10 slow breaths.

Shining Skull Breathing

This vigorous breathing technique from yoga clears your mind, invigorates your respiratory system and generally energizes you. It is something of a physical and mental tonic! Used before meditation, it increases alertness and focus.

Sit on the floor or on a chair with your spine long and straight. Close your eyes and, with one hand on your chest and the other on your abdomen, focus on the rhythm of your breathing and the passage of your breath through your body. Visualize oxygen entering your body through your nostrils and watch it flow through your lungs and into your bloodstream and energize your cells. As you breathe out, visualize waste flowing out of your body — not just carbon dioxide, but also tiredness, anxiety and any negative thoughts. Do this visualization for two or three minutes.

Inhale and, as you breathe out through your nose, contract your abdominal muscles sharply and repeatedly so that you make little repeated exhalations. The aim is to build up to 20 rhythmic, pumping exhalations. This will take time. After Shining Skull Breathing, take two or three normal breaths and then repeat the Shining Skull Breathing five times.

Developing the Crown Chakra

By definition, the crown chakra is intangible – rather than being physical, it is pure spirit. The two main ways to access and develop the crown chakra are meditation and visualization. Using crystals can also help, especially those that are clear and reflect light.

Working with Crystals

Crystals, like chakras, resonate with energy and so you can use them either for healing or as a focus for meditation. The crown chakra has three colours – gold, violet and white. In terms of crystals, clear stones, such as clear quartz, tourmaline or even diamond – the ultimate symbol of clarity and perfection – are the best to work with. These stones reflect the clarity of the chakra itself. When you are choosing crystals, trust your instinct and pick the ones that instantly appeal or call to you.

To use a crystal for healing, hold it near your crown chakra and visualize its power cleansing and healing you. Repeat in your mind an affirmation, such as "I am healed by the spirit of this crystal." You can also wear your crystal or place it under your pillow at night.

CRYSTAL PREPARATION

When you have bought your crystals, get to know them by handling and looking at them. When you are ready to work with them, do the following cleansing ritual. This will strengthen your affinity with the crystals.

1 Leave your crystal (or crystals) for 24 hours in salt water, then place it on a windowsill overnight where it can absorb the moon's beams. The following day, leave the crystal in a place where it will absorb the rays of the sun.

2 Ring a bell or sound some small cymbals over the crystal three times.

3 Burn a bunch of dried herbs and waft the smoke over the crystal.

4 After the cleansing process, you dedicate the crystal to its use. Decide what function you want it to perform or how you want it to help you and, holding the crystal in cupped palms (the right hand on top of the left), state the dedication out loud – for example, "I dedicate this crystal to meditation." Wash crystals regularly in running water and repeat the cleansing and dedication ritual.

CRYSTAL MEDITATION

This meditation is designed to open up the crown chakra and allow divine inspiration to fill your mind and body. You should lie on the floor in warm clothes or with a blanket covering you – remember your temperature always drops during meditation. Place your chosen crystal next to the crown of your head so that you are just in contact with it and aware of its presence. As with all the guided meditations, you may wish to record this one in advance. If so, speak slowly and calmly and leave a pause between the descriptions of each chakra.

1 Lie on the floor with your arms a little away from your sides, your neck and shoulders relaxed and your spine straight. Close your eyes. Let your legs roll out to the sides and feel all of your muscles relax.

2 Starting at your feet, let them soften and sink into the floor. Work your way up your calves, your knees and your thighs, letting them all soften and sink into the floor. Let your buttocks relax and the whole length of your back sink into the floor. Relax your abdominal muscles. Let your chest soften and open, and relax your throat, facial muscles, jaw and head. Let your tongue rest just behind your front teeth.

3 Now turn your focus to the chakras, seeing each of them in turn as a lotus flower. See the root chakra as a lotus with four deep, red petals, pointing downward between your legs, opening to receive the earth's healing energy.

4 Take your focus to the sacral chakra where the healing energy rises to the lotus flower and opens its six orange petals to the sky.

5 Now let the energy flow to the solar plexus chakra. See the ten bright yellow petals of this chakra open to the sun.

6 The energy now reaches the heart chakra. Watch as it opens the heart's lotus flower of twelve green petals.

7 Now turn your focus to the throat chakra where the lotus flower's sixteen sky-blue petals open.

8 The energy now rises to the brow chakra and the two white petals of its lotus flower open.

9 Finally, the energy rises to the crown chakra where the thousand golden petals of its lotus flower open. Your crystal draws down divine light and it flows into the crown chakra and through the sushumna nadi (see page 10) to each of the chakras so that their lotus flowers shine with pure, clear colour. Enjoy this feeling of clarity and light.

10 Gradually, close the thousand lotus petals of the crown chakra, but be aware of the light that still fills your entire being. Allow the lotus flowers to resume their normal shape, but continue to be full of light.

11 Slowly, return to an awareness of your physical body. Allow yourself to rest before returning to your day.

Creating a Sacred Space

You may like to create your own sacred meditation space. This can be a room or just a corner of a table.

If you can dedicate a room to spiritual practice, choose one that has plenty of natural light, is quiet and in which you have a sense of peace and tranquillity. Decorate it with clear colours, and pictures, photographs or objects that have meaning to you.

If you have only a small space, create an altar. Decorate it with objects that help spiritual practice, such as crystals, silks of clear colours, flowers, bowls of water and inspirational pictures.

Crown Chakra Meditation

Meditating on the crown chakra links your mind with the cleansing energy of pure spirit. Allow yourself to connect and accept this purification and, every time you do this meditation, a little more of the negativity to which we all cling will float away, bringing a feeling of wholeness and completeness.

The crown chakra is not really of the body at all. It is the chakra of the spirit, of vision, of purity and of the connection with the divine. One of the recurring themes within Buddhism is the cleansing of the mind – ridding it of the anger and attachments that hold it back from becoming one with the divine, and achieving enlightenment. You might feel jealous, guilty, unlovable or inadequate, but in Buddhism all such feelings are seen as transient. They are just a form of mental energy that has become negative. They are not your true spirit and you can transform this energy into compassion, wisdom or kindness. The purification meditation on the opposite page helps you to banish these negative emotions and to fill your mind and body with divine light.

When you do the purification meditation, allow yourself to experience the emptiness of all harmful and confused states of mind. Feel that these mental delusions are dissolved and destroyed by the purifying light. Try to feel the infinite bliss of this pure, clear state both physically and mentally, and concentrate on it for as long as you can.

You will find, over time, that the clarity that comes from this meditation will impinge increasingly on your day-to-day life, giving you insight into solving problems and creating an underlying feeling of serenity and contentment.

PURIFICATION MEDITATION

This is a powerful, cleansing and purifying meditation that rids you of negative or destructive thoughts and thought patterns. It also allows you to connect with the divine. Do this meditation in your sacred space or in front of your altar (see page 125).

Sit in a comfortable meditation position (see page 119), with your back straight, and supported if necessary. Begin by focusing on your breath. Take a long, deep breath in, feeling the life-giving oxygen flood your body and then leave it, taking away the waste that your body does not need. Repeat this three times.

Breathe normally and on every out-breath, visualize all of the negativity in your life — harmful and painful emotions, poor self-esteem, the mistakes you have made — leave your body along with your breath. Visualize your out-breath as a dark smoke that, as it leaves your body, disperses and evaporates. Feel yourself free of all the negativity that you have been clinging to.

As you breathe in, feel the pure energy of the divine fill you with light. Let it flow with the oxygen into your lungs, through your bloodstream and into every cell of your body. This energy brings clarity, wisdom and bliss. Focus on your light-filled mind and body. If any thoughts or feelings come to distract you, don't follow them. They are simply random pulses of your energy. Breathe them out with the smoke and return to your enlightened being. Now visualize the light dissolving all of the cells of your body so that you are made of nothing but divine light. Enjoy this blissful feeling of becoming as one with the divine, universal energy. Let yourself blaze with light.

You are now experiencing your own true divine energy; your own true perfection. All of the negative feelings and thoughts that previously held you back have left you, and you have become part of the universal light. Shine with this light for as long as you can, then, when you are ready, start to visualize your material body recreating itself within the light. Let your body recreate itself afresh, made of divine energy. Gradually come back to your body, finally focusing on your breath. Stay focused on your breath for a few minutes and then dedicate your renewed positive energy to the enlightenment of all beings. Take this knowledge of your true divine self with you as you go back to your normal day.

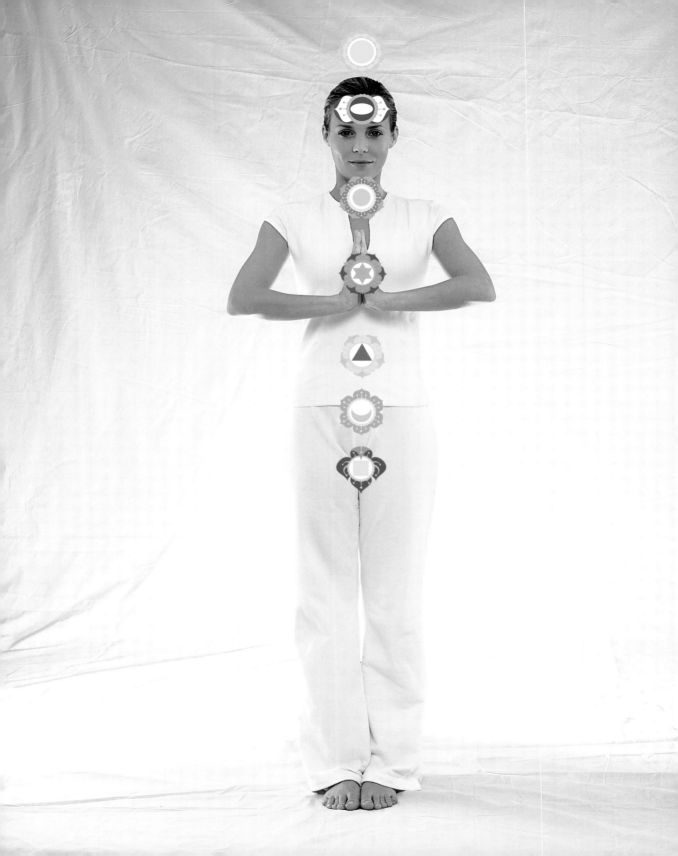

Chakras in Balance

Each chakra is unique – it resonates at a particular frequency, is represented by a specific colour and comprises a particular aspect of our being. But despite their uniqueness, the chakras form an energetic holistic system, and for this system to work well there needs to be balance and harmony in each individual chakra.

If you spend too much time working on one chakra, you may block or restrict the flow of energy to another chakra. Rather than correcting an imbalance, this brings about a new imbalance. Your aim should always be to bring all the chakras into balance, creating a profound sense of harmony – this harmony is a gift that you can offer back to the universe.

A Balanced System

Life is all about change. Nothing stays the same for a moment, whether it is the internal state of our bodies or the outside environment. We and the world are in a constant state of movement and change. The chakras reflect this by changing all the time too.

The chakras consist of pure vibrational energy and they are constantly opening, closing and exchanging energy. When we talk of balancing the chakras, this is not a finite process. The balancing process needs to go on continuously throughout our lives. Chakra energy is affected by many factors. Even on a day-to-day basis, the things that happen to us can affect the balance between the chakras, placing emphasis or stress on a particular chakra. For example, delivering an important speech places emphasis on your throat chakra, which controls verbal communication.

Sometimes a particular chakra needs to dominate so that you can deal with whatever challenge you are facing. For example, when you are confronted with a physical challenge, especially one in which you feel your survival is threatened, it is important that your root chakra takes over – the root chakra governs the fight-or-flight response, which enables you to take fast action in an emergency. However, the problem is that when one chakra dominates all the time, it can take over and block the energy of the other chakras. This throws the whole system out of balance.

Some chakra imbalances go back a long way and can be difficult to address. Imbalances that arise from childhood can be particularly hard to resolve. A child who was starved of love and affection will generally have a blocked heart chakra. A child who was told to "be seen and not heard" is likely to have a blocked throat chakra and be unable to express himself. According to Buddhist philosophy, we are also born with karmic imbalances that result from mistakes we have made in earlier incarnations. Or, in other words, the baggage that we are carrying from previous lives.

Whatever the cause of imbalance, the aim of this book is to create a chakra system where energy flows freely and uninterruptedly between all of the chakras. While you will want to work on specific problems that you can identify with particular chakras, it is important never to lose sight of the optimum equilibrium you are aiming for in all seven chakras. For a true sense of well-being and fulfilment, each chakra must be in a state of harmony with the others. Practising the yoga postures that follow in this chapter can help you to achieve this harmony.

Yoga to Balance the Chakras

This sequence of yoga postures is called Salute to the Sun – Surya Namaskar in Sanskrit. It is one of the most unifying and balancing sequences in yoga and will help to bring your chakras into balance. You can perform the sequence quickly or slowly and you can make it more vigorous by jumping instead of stepping from position to position.

Salute to the Sun

Salute to the Sun is a perfect start to any yoga practice as it brings all of your chakras into balance and warms up all of your muscles at the same time. This is a fairly simple version of the sequence, but if you go to a yoga class, your teacher will give you advice about how to develop Salute to the Sun further. Do five complete rounds.

1 Stand with your feet together in a long, strong posture with no tension in your shoulders or neck, and your hands together in prayer position.

2 Breathe in and stretch your arms up to the ceiling with your palms together. Bend back if you can do so without strain.

3 Breathe out and bend forward, folding over your legs and taking your head toward your knees. Place your hands on your ankles or feet, or on the floor by your feet.

4 Breathe in and lift your head to look forward.

5 Breathe out and step or jump back so that your body is supported in one long line on your hands and toes.

6 Breathe out and lower your knees and chest to the floor. Breathe in, roll your toes over so that your feet are pointed and lift your body up, arching your back if you can do so without strain.

7 Breathe out, roll your toes back and raise your hips to the ceiling into Downward-facing Dog (see page 56).

8 Breathe in and jump or step your feet forward to meet your hands. Grasp your ankles or calves. Raise your head to look up.

9 Breathe out and bend forward, folding over your legs with your head toward your knees.

10 Breathe in, return to standing with your arms stretched above your head, palms together. Breathe out and return to position 1.

ULTIMATE RELAXATION

The final exercise of this book brings you into a place of complete stillness, relaxation and peace. This in turn helps to bring all of the chakras into balance and harmony. The exercise is from yoga and it is known as yoga nidra, or "deep sleep". You can do yoga nidra before or after meditation. It is also a good way to refresh you during the day, and to help relax you in the evening, preparing you for a sound night's sleep. Yoga nidra is done lying in the yoga Corpse Pose on the floor (not on a bed, because you may become too relaxed and fall asleep!). Corpse Pose is a deeply relaxing pose that stills and centres your mind and body. It is known in Sanskrit as Savasana. Rather than trying to remember the relaxation sequence as you do the exercise (not very relaxing!), record it in advance, speaking slowly and calmly and leaving plenty of pauses between each of the stages. There are lots of repetitions because you need time to focus on each particular part of the body. The whole recording, including the pauses, should last between 30 and 40 minutes. Alternatively, ask someone you know to guide you through yoga nidra, reading the instructions on the opposite page aloud in a clear, calm voice.

Corpse Pose

Lie on your back. Cover yourself with a blanket and put socks on if you think you may get cold. Check that your neck and shoulders are relaxed and that your spine is one long straight line. Your neck forms part of this line and you will need to tilt your chin down slightly for the right alignment. Let your legs and arms fall open and relax. Turn your palms to face upward. Close your eyes and breathe deeply from your abdomen, feeling the air fill your whole body. Rest in this position for several minutes. Now you are ready to start yoga nidra.

Yoga Nidra – Deep Sleep

Focus your attention on your left foot. Become aware of your left foot. Take your awareness into your toes.

Become aware of your big toe. Feel your big toe soften and relax.

Become aware of your second toe. Feel it soften and relax.

Become aware of your third toe. Feel it soften and relax.

Become aware of your fourth toe. Feel it soften and relax.

Become aware of your little toe. Feel it soften and relax.

All your toes are soft and relaxed.

Take your awareness into the sole of the foot. It is relaxing. Your left sole is relaxed.

Take your awareness into your left heel. It is relaxing. Your left heel is relaxed.

Take your awareness into the top of your foot. It is relaxing. The top of your foot is relaxed.

Become aware of your left ankle. It is relaxing. Your left ankle is relaxed.

Become aware of your left calf, your calf muscle, your shin and knee. Your left calf is relaxing. It has become relaxed. The shin is relaxing. It has become relaxed. Your left knee is relaxing. It has become relaxed.

Let your awareness flow up toward your thigh. Feel the muscles in the front of your thigh relaxing. They are relaxed. Feel the muscles in the back of your thigh relaxing. They are relaxed.

Let your awareness travel up to your left buttock. Feel the muscles relaxing. They are relaxed.

The whole of your left leg, from your toes to the buttock is now relaxed.

Now repeat this whole sequence for your right leg.

Become aware of your abdomen. Become aware of how it rises and falls. Your abdomen is relaxing. Your breathing is relaxing. Your abdomen is relaxed.

Focus your awareness on your pelvic area. Become aware of your sexual organs, your bladder, and your colon. Feel them all relaxing. The whole pelvic area is relaxed.

Become aware of your back. Feel your lower back, your middle back and your upper back against the floor. Feel your lower back, your middle back, your upper back relaxing. Your whole back is relaxed.

Become aware of your chest. Become aware of it rising and falling. Feel your lungs soften and relax. Feel your chest soften and relax. The whole of your chest is relaxed.

Take your attention to your left hand.

Become aware of your little finger. Feel it soften and relax.

Become aware of your next finger. Feel it soften and relax.

Become aware of your middle finger. Feel it soften and relax.

Become aware of your index finger. Feel it soften and relax.

Become aware of your thumb. Feel it soften and relax. All your fingers are relaxed.

Become aware of your palm. Your palm is relaxing. It is relaxed.

Become aware of the back of your hand. The back of your hand is relaxing. It is relaxed.

Become aware of your wrist. Your wrist is relaxing. It is relaxed.

Become aware of your forearm, front and back. It is relaxing. It is relaxed.

Become aware of your elbow. Your elbow is relaxing. It is relaxed.

Become aware of your upper arm. It is relaxing. It is relaxed.

Become aware of your left shoulder. It is relaxing. It is relaxed.

The whole of your left arm from your fingers to your shoulder is relaxed.

Now repeat this whole sequence for your right arm.

Let your focus float upward to your throat and neck. They are relaxing. Your throat and neck are relaxed.

Become aware of your face: jaw, chin, cheeks, nose, lips. They are all relaxing. Your mouth, tongue and lips are all relaxing.

Become aware of your left eye, the eyelid, the eyebrow. They are all relaxing.

Become aware of your right eye, the eyelid, the eyebrow. They are all relaxing.

Become aware of your brow. It is relaxing. Your brow is relaxed. The whole of your face is relaxed.

Become aware of your ears. Your ears are relaxing. They are relaxed.

Become aware of your head, your scalp. The whole of your scalp is relaxing. The whole of your head is relaxed.

Become aware of your whole body and mind. Feel your body as light as your breath, floating in a state of total relaxation. Feel your mind relaxed but aware. You are in a state of yoga nidra.

Pause for three minutes at this point.

Become aware of the lightness of your breath and the way in which your breath enters and leaves your body.

Lie on the floor for at least five minutes, as you return to normal consciousness.

Conclusion

The exercises and suggestions I have given in this book are designed to start you on a path to realising your own unique potential. This path will be different for each person who reads this book. Everyone will begin from his or her own starting point and with a different set of aims in mind. You may find that as you work through the book, you develop an interest in yoga or chi gong that you would like to take further. Or perhaps you will want to explore a therapy such as massage, or learn how to still the mind by taking up a regular meditation practice.

Whatever journey you make, I hope that by working on the chakras, you achieve at least two things. The first is an understanding that you are not alone – that you can connect to a greater, universal energy of which you are an integral part. This energy will support you in life. In this context, try to picture the chakras functioning as funnels of energy that draw on universal energy. This universal energy is always there and you can use it to heal and cleanse your mind, body and spirit.

However, the chakras can also be understood in a quite different way. All too often, guilt, low self-esteem, a fear of failure – or of success – holds us back. We may be afraid to show our emotions in case they are rejected. We may stay locked into unfulfilling relationships, jobs or situations because we lack the confidence to take a step into the unknown. We may ignore our spirituality because it seems out of step with the materialist world of the 21st century. There may simply be parts of ourselves that we dislike or of which we feel ashamed.

So my second aim in writing this book is that you start to relate to the chakras as representations or symbols that stand for the many different elements of you and that, together, make up your essential self. By understanding, restoring and celebrating each in turn, I hope that this process gives you a greater knowledge of and love for yourself. We are all composed of pure universal energy – our true Buddha natures. We just have to allow this energy to shine through.

Treating Specific Ailments

Particular health problems are linked to imbalances in particular chakras. These may be problems related to your physical health or to your emotional/mental health. By working on the chakra that is linked to your specific problem, you can help to alleviate or overcome the problem. Always use both the mind and body exercises (yoga, chi gong and meditation) in the relevant chapter – a holistic approach always works best.

Ailment	Chakra
Addictive behaviour	root, solar plexus
Aggression	solar plexus
Allergies	solar plexus, heart
Asthma	heart, throat
Back pain	root, sacral
Bladder problems	sacral
Constipation	root
Cystitis	sacral
Depression	root, crown
Diabetes	solar plexus
Digestive problems	solar plexus
Dyslexia	brow
Ear infections	throat
Epilepsy	crown
Eye problems	brow
Fatigue	root, heart, crown
Fertility problems	sacral
Fibroids	sacral
Food allergies	solar plexus
Frigidity/impotence	sacral
Gallstones	solar plexus
Glaucoma	brow

Gynecological problems	sacral
Hemorrhoids	root
Headaches	throat, brow
Hearing problems	throat
Heart problems	heart
Immune disorders	sacral, heart
Inability to express yourself	throat
Inability to make commitment	heart
Insomnia	brow
High blood pressure	heart
Learning difficulties	brow
Loneliness	sacral
Loss of voice	throat
Lung problems	heart
Kidney problems	solar plexus
Knee problems	root
Liver problems	solar plexus
Mouth ulcers	throat
Muscle cramps	sacral
Nightmares	brow
Obesity	root
Osteoarthritis	root
Over-sensitivity	solar plexus
Prostate problems	sacral
Rheumatism	root
Sadness	heart
Sciatica	root
Self-esteem problems	solar plexus
Sexual problems	sacral
Sore throats	throat
Teeth and gum conditions	throat
Thyroid problems	throat
Tinnitus	throat
Ulcers	solar plexus

Index

Acknowledgments

Picture credits

The publisher would like to thank the following photographic libraries for permission to reproduce their material. Every care has been taken to trace copyright holders. However, if we have omitted anyone, we apologise and will, if informed, make corrections in any future edition.

page 29 Laura Lane/Getty Images;
page 45 DomPassy/Photolibrary.com;
page 77 Julie Toy/Getty Images;
page 109 Altrendo Nature/Getty Images.

Models
Fiona Brattle
Jasmine Hemsley
Jennifer Young

Make-up artists
Gilly Popham
Angela Lea Phair